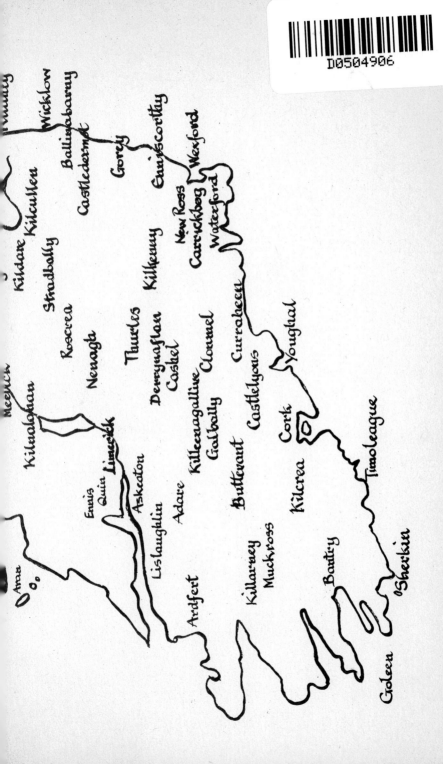

FRANCISCAN IRELAND

The story of seven hundred and fifty years of the Friars Minor in Ireland . . . with notes on all the major sites associated with the friars . . . and a brief description of the other members of the Franciscan family in Ireland.

PATRICK CONLAN O.F.M.

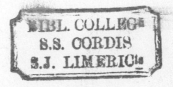
THE MERCIER PRESS
DUBLIN and CORK

THE MERCIER PRESS, 4 Bridge Street, Cork
25 Lower Abbey Street, Dublin 1

ISBN 0 85342 514 0

Nihil obstat: Fr Cathaldus Giblin o.f.m., Censor deputatus.
Imprimi potest: Fr Louis Brennan o.f.m., Minister Provincialis.

Acknowledgements:

The jacket is an adaptation, by Linda Maguire, Athlone, of a sixteenth century bas-relief, 'St Francis and the birds', in the ruins of Creevelea friary. The drawings in this book were done by her, and by Maureen Purcell and Frances Delahunty of the South Tipperary Art Group, Clonmel. The map is the work of Sr Bernard of the Sainte Union Sisters, Athlone. Aileen Coughlan and Frances Duffy helped me to correct the text. My sincere thanks to all. The photograph of Ross friary is reproduced by permission of the Commissioners of Public Works in Ireland.

CONTENTS

Dromahair Friary: Flower Finial

PREFACE

Paul-Marie Duval of the Institut de France recently wrote that Celtic literature reveals a taste for the supernatural, a poetry of dreams and of fairy-like enchantment, and a quality of unreality which is in complete contrast to Mediterranean classicism. The art of the Celts breaks with the symmetry of classical models in its display of a freedom of invention which reflects the Celt's independence of mind and his constant revolt against conformity. The Celtic Gods were Gods of nature — cosmic forces, rivers, mountains, animals . . . (cf. The UNESCO Courier, Dec. 1975). If you consider the matter a little, you will see that this Celtic insight shares quite a lot with the basic Franciscan vision — a stress on the poetic and the artistic rather than on the scientific and the rigorous, on the individual rather than the group, and on the goodness of creation rather than the inventions of men.

The early Franciscans first met the Celtic mentality in Ireland and the two recognised in each other kindred souls. After a few years of hesitation, the Irish saw in Franciscanism a reflection of their own deep sentiments. This identification was further cemented during the tremendous Irish resurgence of the fifteenth century and was completed with the unification of the themes of faith and fatherland towards the close of the following century. Franciscanism is still a religious tradition closely identified with the Irish spirit.

This book seeks to fulfil a long-felt need for a general history of and a reference work on Irish Franciscanism. It is mainly the story of the Irish Province of the Order of Friars Minor, with short sections on the other branches of the Franciscan family in Ireland. Much of the earlier material can be found in print elsewhere, but has been integrated here into a continuous story. Little of the history from 1750 on has been published previously. When individual items have been inserted into their historical context, we can discover an orderly flow of events. We gain a greater appreciation of our past. In judging other generations we realise the historicity of our own actions.

I am aware of the danger of generalisation, but I feel that this risk has to be taken in presenting a first look at 750 years of continuous Irish Franciscan history. I wish to thank the many friars who have encouraged me in this project. This book is a product, not only of my own work, but also of the co-operation of many people, to whom I am very grateful.

9

Chapter 1

THE FRIARS COME AND SETTLE
IN IRELAND (1226 ? – 1291)

About seven hundred and fifty years ago, probably in the summer
of 1226, a ship arrived at the mouth of the Blackwater, just off the
port of Youghal. Among the tired passengers was a group of men
dressed in poor grey habits, but whose richness of spirit over-
shadowed their poverty. The harbingers of the Franciscan ideal had
arrived on the shores of Ireland.

Unfortunately we know very little about these early arrivals except
for oral tradition written down long after. The friary at Youghal has
always been recognised as the first foundation of the Franciscans in
Ireland. This event must be dated between the arrival of the friars in
England in 1224 and the General Chapter of the Order at Assisi in
1230. According to one tradition these friars were Romantics from
the sunny Mediterranean, coming to Ireland via N. Spain. It seems
much more likely that they were Norman-French who came across St
George's Channel from southern England. In any case, they would
have found Ireland a strange country. While the townspeople could
converse with them in the sort of bastard French spoken over much
of 'civilised' Europe, the natives spoke an unkown language and lived
according to their own strange laws and customs.

The Franciscans in England and Scotland

The well-documented history of the early Franciscans in England
gives us an idea of how the friars spread through Ireland. A group of
friars would come to a town and find a residence for themselves.
Then the main group would move on, leaving behind the nucleus of a
new community. Thus, the first English friars landed at Dover and
formed their first community at Canterbury on 11th. Sept. 1224. The
main body then moved on to London, from where the friars rapidly
spread to Oxford and Northampton. By 1230 sufficient friars had
penetrated into Scotland for it to be erected as a full province. In
1239 Scotland was reduced to a dependent vicariate of the English
Province, but it remained a fairly independent unit until it vanished
with the collapse of Franciscanism in England during the
Reformation.

Expansion in Ireland: a full province

After their arrival at Youghal, it would seem that the friars split
into three groups. Two small groups set off to make foundations at
Cork and Waterford. A larger group went to Kilkenny and thence to

11

Dublin. From there, some went to Athlone, while others continued on up the coast to Drogheda, Downpatrick and Carrickfergus. During the next few years gaps between the early foundations were filled with houses at New Ross, Castledermot and Dundalk. Local rulers invited the friars to come to Ardfert and Claregalway. Armagh, the religious centre of Ireland, was next on the Franciscan list. Then it was the turn of the towns of Munster: Nenagh, Limerick, Cashel and Ennis. Finally, before the end of the century, came foundations at Buttevant and Clonmel in the South; Wexford and Wicklow in the East; Trim, Kildare, Clane, Multyfarnham and Killeigh in the Midlands; and Galway in the West. While the exact chronological order may be a matter of dispute, the friars had made a total of thirty foundations in a period of just over sixty years.

As the number of houses grew, the time became opportune for the creation of an independent Irish Province within the Franciscan Order. This was done at or before the General Chapter held at Assisi during Pentecost 1230. The Chapter was to be the occasion for the solemn translation of the body of St Francis to the new Basilica built by Br Elias. But relics were valuable in those far-off days, and the body of St Francis was hidden, lest it be stolen, until 1818, when it was found in a pillar in the lower crypt of the Basilica. At the Chapter Fr John Parenti was elected Minister General to replace Br Elias. He appointed Richard of Ingworth as the first Minister Provincial of the Irish Franciscan Province.

Ingworth is a village about ten miles north of Norwich. Richard, an experienced administrator, was said to have been one of the first friars to preach north of the Alps. A member of the first group of friars in England, he founded the friary at Northampton. He later became Custos of Northern England, based at Cambridge. He acted as locum for Agnellus of Pisa when the latter went to the General Chapter in 1230. Agnellus was a much respected friar, so we may see his hand in the appointment of Richard to Ireland. Little is known of his activities in Ireland as Provincial. What we do know is that he was involved in a rather difficult visitation of the Scottish Province in 1238, and when his period of office ended at the General Chapter of 1239, Richard went as a missionary to Syria, where he died.

The next Irish Provincial was a former Provincial of Scotland, John Keating, a native of Ketton in Rutland. He was appointed to Ireland in 1239 by the new Minister General, Albert of Pisa, himself ex-Provincial of England. Friar John had such a reputation for kindness that friars from many provinces came to Ireland seeking his protection. The first known Provincial Chapter was held under him at Cork in 1244. He purchased a bible for the Irish Province at Paris in 1251. He was replaced at the General Chapter at Metz in 1254.

The life of the early friars

One became a friar in those days by going to the nearest friary, where one could be admitted to the novitiate in a matter of days. Sometimes there were problems, as when the Earl of Ulster, Walter de Burgo, sent an armed band to remove his young brother, Daniel, from the novitiate in Dublin friary in 1258.

The friary itself was hardly more than a collection of huts around a stone chapel donated by some willing citizen. As time went on, the friars added to the original structure until the whole formed one of those buildings whose romantic ruins decorate the Irish countryside. Sometimes a local ruler invited the friars to come and he himself built a house for them. In many cases the friary grounds became the burial place of the local family, e.g. the O'Briens in Ennis and Limerick, the FitzMaurice family in Kildare and the O'Driscolls on Sherkin Island. The Crown in England was also a major benefactor to many friaries. It is often impossible to give a precise date for the arrival of the friars in a particular area. Some sources give the date of arrival, others the date of the initial foundation, and yet others the date of the major benefaction. The result can be confusing.

The main work of the friars, in addition to bearing witness to a particular style of Christian living, was preaching. As early as 1240 we find them preaching a Crusade and forwarding the money for this to Rome. It is significant that the earliest known Franciscan writing in Ireland, the *Liber Exemplorum*, is a collection of notes and stories for preachers. It was written about 1270 by an English friar who was stationed in Ireland. He knew Drogheda, Cork and Dublin, and was obviously a much travelled man. One of his stories concerns fertility rites in northern Germany as related to the Dublin community by a Danish friar.

Travel was much more common in those days than we imagine. Two friars, Simon Fitz Simeon and Hugo the Illuminator, journeyed from Ireland to the Holy Land. They went via Anglesea, London, Dover, Wissant, Paris, the Rhone, Marseilles, Bobbio, Venice and Alexandria to Jerusalem. Hugo died at Alexandria on the 22nd. Oct. 1324. There is also a tradition that a Friar James of Ireland accompanied Blessed Odoric of Pordenone to China in 1316-1320.

There are a number of other Irish Franciscan writings of the same period in addition to the *Liber Exemplorum*. An Anglo-Irish friar made a collection of French, English and Latin songs and poems in Munster about 1325; the *Annals of Nenagh* and the *Annals of Friar John Clyn* of Kilkenny were written about 1350. Finally there is a mysterious theological treatise on the seven deadly sins, *De Veneno*, usually attributed to a Friar Malachy of Limerick and dated about 1285.

13

Fr Thomas Quin was the first Irish Franciscan to be elected (not simply appointed) to an Irish bishopric. This was in the diocese of Elphin, but he was not confirmed to the see by the king. Following another election and after a dispensation had been obtained, since he was the son of a priest, he was consecrated bishop of Clonmacnoise in 1252. An interesting side-light on the relationship between the friars and the bishops is provided by the request made by Bishop Maurice of Ross in 1265 that he be allowed to relinquish his see in order to join the friars, and do penance for his misdeeds and maladministration.

The beginning of the problem of the two nations

In the beginning, the Franciscans in Ireland worked mainly among the Norman townspeople. The Provincials were generally of English birth, although a Gilbert of Slane (or Clane) held that office about 1266. The Franciscan charism is all-embracing, and the friars soon began to mix with the Irish. Inevitably they were caught up in the politics of the two nations in Ireland: the Irish nation and the English nation. Thus a Franciscan bishop of Kildare, Nicholas Cusack, reported to King Edward I: 'The peace of the land is frequently disturbed by secret counsels . . . which certain insolent religious of Irish tongue . . . hold with the Irish. Thus in dangerous districts Irish sympathisers should be removed from their convents and replaced by good and carefully selected English'. The report of a Royal Commission in 1284-85 is more explicit: 'The Dominicans and Franciscans make too much use of that (Irish) language'.

This problem of the two nations remained a major difficulty for two centuries. The English authorities ran a European-style church. They used their contacts with Rome to advantage, so that Irish bishops had to obtain the Royal consent before they were consecrated. But the old Celtic church remained on in the Irish areas, admittedly with a Roman flavour since the reforms of the twelfth century. In practice the two nations solved their problems by keeping apart. There is little evidence of dissension at local level among the Franciscans, but there was a struggle for control of the Province itself.

A Provincial Chapter opened in Cork on 10th. June 1291 to which some of the friars came armed with Papal Bulls. A Chronicler of the subsequent events remarks: 'Papal Bulls always excite men'. The issue was control of the Province. Initially the Irish won by force of numbers. Then fighting broke out. The Anglo-Irish townspeople came to the rescue of their fellow friars. Sixteen friars were killed. Curiously the Minister General, a Frenchman named

Raymond Godefrey, happened to arrive soon after on one of his long voyages through Europe. The result of his visit was drastic. A decision was taken that the Irish could not be trusted to rule themselves. Within a couple of years direct rule from Rome was introduced. For the next one hundred and sixty years, the Irish Provincial was appointed by Rome and was always of English or Anglo-Irish stock.

Askeaton Friary: St Francis

Chapter 2

A LONG PERIOD OF CONSOLIDATION (1291 – 1460)

After an initial burst of creative energy, the Irish friars settled down to a period of consolidation. There were few new foundations, although existing houses were extended. Some local rulers invited the friars to found houses in their territories. New friaries were built at Carrickbeg, Cavan, Monasteroris and Timoleague. The Franciscans took over the only Irish Carthusian foundation at Kilnalahan.

The invasion by Edward Bruce

When Edward Bruce landed in Ireland in May 1315, Franciscan reaction was mixed. Within a month of his arrival, his forces had sacked Dundalk friary. Yet support for him grew among the Irish friars. On the other side, the English king, Edward II, appealed to Rome for a condemnation of his opponent. The Irish Franciscan Provincial, Thomas Godman, was sent to the Pope. He was accompanied by Geoffrey of Aylsham, a politically reliable Franciscan of English blood and the royal nominee for the vacant see of Cashel. Action in Rome was slowed by the delay in the election of Pope John XXII. During the delay, Castledermot friary was burned in 1317. In reply to the king, a group of Irish chieftains sent a Remonstrance, sometimes taken as the first expression of Irish nationalism, to the Pope in 1318. Among other things, this document accuses an Anglo-Irish friar of claiming that 'it is no sin to kill a man of Irish birth and, if he did such a thing, he would not hesitate from celebrating mass'. In the end the Pope took the diplomatic way out. While condemning Bruce, John XXII rejected the nomination of Geoffrey for Cashel.

The two nations: attempts at separation

The problem of the two nations in Ireland underlies most of the history of the fourteenth century. One solution tried within the Irish Franciscans was the division of the Province into four or five administrative units called custodies. The composition of each one was fluid. While one custody was always Irish, the others were always Anglo-Irish.

The division of the custodies in 1331 was as follows:

Custody of Nenagh (Irish): Nenagh, Armagh, Athlone, Cavan, Claregalway, Ennis, Galway & Killeigh.
Custody of Dublin (Anglo-Irish): Dublin, Castledermot, Clane, Kildare, Monasteroris, Wexford & Wicklow.

16

Custody of Cork (Anglo-Irish): Cork, Ardfert, Buttevant, Limerick, & Timoleague.

Custody of Cashel (Anglo-Irish): Cashel, Clonmel, Kilkenny, New Ross, Waterford & Youghal.

Custody of Drogheda (Anglo-Irish): Drogheda, Carrickfergus, Downpatrick, Dundalk, Multyfarnham & Trim.

Given the political conditions, it is not surprising that the civil authorities tried to restrict the entry of the Irish into religious orders under certain circumstances. Thus a parliament at Kilkenny in 1310 ordered a complete prohibition on the reception of Irish into religious orders in the 'terre Engleis', the area governed by the English. Fortunately this particular statute was rapidly revoked.

The problem of the political reliability of the Irish is seen among the Franciscans at the Provincial Chapter which met in Dublin in 1324. Special judges appointed by the Pope found that the conduct of the friars in Cork, Limerick, Buttevant, Ardfert, Nenagh, Claregalway, Galway and Athlone was politically suspect. The Chapter decreed that no Irishman could be guardian of one of these houses and all Irish friars, except for some of the most trustworthy, were to be removed from them. In practice it would seem that the rules were not applied too strictly, yet the authorities kept a watch. The royal alms for Athlone was transferred to Cashel in 1327, since the Athlone friars could no longer be trusted. Thus three years after the supposed exclusion of unloyal friars from Athlone in 1324, there were no longer sufficient loyal friars in the community! This problem of the two nations remained until the next century, and reached a high point in the Statutes of Kilkenny in 1366. It slowly vanished as the two nations began to fuse more and more until it was submerged by the Irish resurgence from 1450 on.

The life and work of the friars

By this time, the friars had become well established. Quite a number became bishops. Examples would be Dr Michael Maglachlyn of Derry (1319-24), Dr Robert le Petit of Annaghdown (1325-28), Dr Thomas de Brakenbergh of Leighlin (1349-60) and Dr Bernard O'Connor of Ross, later of Limerick (1379-98). Perhaps the most famous Irish Franciscan bishop of this period was Dr Richard Ledred of Ossory, whose tomb may still be seen in Kilkenny. Since he was an Englishman and a member of the English Province, the king had no difficulty in confirming the appointment as a bishop. Seemingly consecrated by Pope John XXII, Richard began his career full of enthusiasm. He called synods, promulgated statutes, restored the cathedral, reformed the liturgy, etc. Then he came up against Alice Kettle and her son William Outlaw. Richard accused them of a variety of offences, such as heresy and witch-craft. The diocese was rent assunder in the ensuing disturbances. Under pressure, Bishop Richard fled to England and ended his days in 1360 as a semi-permanent suppliant before the Popes at Avignon.

The normal work of the friars remained that of passive witness and of preaching. Many friary churches were extended. In the middle of the century, their work was interrupted by the Black Death. This broke out on the east coast in Aug. 1348. By December, twenty-five friars had died in Drogheda and twenty-three in Dublin. The friars also evolved their own customs, such as electing superiors by universal vote of the community.

There are few writings by Irish Franciscans of this period extant. However we have evidence of serious work in the area of study. While some rural friaries seem to have had small quasi-bardic schools for secular study, each of the larger friaries probably had its lectors in philosophy and theology. There is evidence for lectors at Ennis, Ardfert, Armagh, Askeaton, Dublin, Nenagh, Limerck, and later at Drogheda and Galway. Some Irish friars studied on the Continent. A Friar Denis of Ireland was at Paris in 1303. Philip Torrington ofm., afterwards Archbishop of Cashel, studied at Oxford and Cambridge. There were two Irish friars at Strasbourg around 1375. Thomas O'Colman ofm., an unsuccessful nominee for the diocese of Armagh, had studied at Paris, Oxford, Cambridge and Lincoln. In 1441 there was one Irish friar at Bologna, three at Cologne and one at Cambridge. The friars had also been involved in the effort to set up a university in Ireland in 1320.

Disputes with the diocesan clergy

As the ordinary friar went about his work, he began to find his interests clashing with those of the diocesan clergy. The usual points at issue were: absolution in reserved cases, permission to preach, the right to quest, the right to bury lay people in friary ground with the resultant problems of benefactions and the seizure of goods. These difficulties first came to a head under Richard FitzRalph, Archbishop of Armagh. Some sources show him as a most holy man and the cause of his beatification was taken up. Others speak of him as 'insidious venom'. In fact, it would seem that he was simply over-zealous. On this occasion the rights of the friars were confirmed when the Decree *Vas electionis* of Pope John XXII (1321) was re-issued in 1359.

The disputes became more serious when John Whitehead, a Master of Theology, supported by the Archbishop of Armagh, began a preaching crusade against the friars. The matter became sufficiently famous to be cited at the University of Paris. Whitehead added a further statement to the usual accusations: 'friars asking the privilege of hearing confessions . . . are in mortal sin by so asking, and a Pope granting such privileges is also in mortal sin and excommunicated; friars are not pastors of the true flock but madmen, thieves and wolves'. The various orders in Ireland formed a league to defend themselves and sent an Augustinian and a Franciscan to the Pope. A condemnation of Whitehead's teachings quickly followed. One reason why such disputes took so long to settle was uncertainty as to the value of certain papal decrees, in particular those of John XXII, due to the Great Western Schism. Any remaining doubts were settled by the Decree *Regnans in excelsis* of Alexander V, issued in October 1409.

The old arguments broke out once more about 1438. The instigator was Master Philip Norreys of Dublin, who had just returned from studying at Oxford. Philip was first condemned by Eugene IV in *Exhibita nobis* (1440) and again by Nicholas V in *Dudum felicis* (1448). He faded into obscurity and died in 1465.

By now the Irish Franciscans had consolidated their position in the country. The Anglo-Normans had been absorbed by the Irish. The friars were structurally well established. It was only natural that the increasing Irish influence would lead to a reform of the Franciscan spirit.

Waterford Friary: Monster

Chapter 3
THE OBSERVANT REFORM IN IRELAND
(1460 — 1540)

We meet the first signs of a new spirit among the Irish Franciscans towards the end of the fourteenth century. Thus permission was obtained for a foundation at Ballabeg in the Isle of Man in 1367. Some Franciscan works written in Irish appear, such as the poems of Tadhg Camchosach (Cruikshanks) Ó Dálaig (floruit c. 1400) and, much later, those of Pilib Bocht Ó hUiginn (died 1487). These poets were just one sign of the Gaelic resurgence which was sweeping the country in the fifteenth century. Another sign is the flamboyant style of architecture which can still be seen in many medieval Franciscan ruins.

A new spirit of Franciscan idealism was growing on the Continent under the guidance of such men as Sts John Capistran and Bernardine of Sienna. They sought a return to the original ideals of St Francis, the Poor Man of Assisi. Their movement, known as the Observant Reform, was first approved by the General Chapter of the Order at Assisi in 1430. The friars who did not share this spirit of reform were known as the Conventuals. Both parties remained within the same Order for nearly a century. The differences eventually became too great and Pope Leo X split the Order into two distinct Orders by the Bull *Ite et Vos* of the 29th. May 1517.

The beginning of the Irish Observants

In Ireland, the desire to lead a stricter form of the Franciscan life and the Gaelic resurgence went hand in hand. From 1400 on, individual friars began to live the newer form of life in remote houses in Irish districts. Individual reformers then came together to form groups. The next obvious step was an actual foundation. Apparently advantage was taken of a permission granted by Eugene IV in 1433 to Sioda Cam MacNamara, chieftain at Quin in Co. Clare, to build a new friary on the remains of a de Clare castle. This was the first actual Observant foundation. The second was at Muckross, near Killarney, founded by the McCarthy family about 1445.

In law both of these new houses remained subject to the Irish Provincial. He was still appointed from outside and was Anglo-Irish. As such he favoured the Conventual party within the Order. Rather than have houses subject to him, the Irish Observants wished to establish communities directly under the Ultramontane Observant Vicar General of the Order. Permission was granted for two such houses in Co.Cork in 1449, but it would seen that these were not built until after 1460. In the interval Moyne was built some time before 1456. On completion it was immediately taken over as the first true Irish Observant friary, subject to the Ultramontane Vicar General.

One other important change took place at about the same time as the Observant Reform got under way. The law by which the Minister Provincial was appointed directly from Rome was altered. Fr William O'Reilly, an Irishman, was appointed Provincial in 1445. He was removed from office in 1448 when the English Court objected that 'our progenitors have ordered that none of Irish blood, name and nation shall be Minister . . . for the numerous mischiefs that before this (they have) caused'. We do not know the details, but Fr William seems to have been re-appointed around 1450 and continued in office until 1471. Towards the end of his term, it becomes obvious that he was elected, not appointed by Rome. This ended a situation which had lasted since the Chapter at Cork in 1291.

Recognition of the Observants

The Irish Observants seem to have been greatly influenced by their French brethren. Communications were slow and the Observant Constitutions of 1451 do not seem to have been known in Ireland. One Irish Observant, Fr Nehemias O'Donohue, attended the rather stormy General Chapter at Rome in 1458. In his absence, the Irish reformers discovered their right to have an Observant Vicar Provincial and elected Fr Malachy O'Clune to the post. At Rome, the newly elected Pope, Pius II, issued a Bull re-organising the Observants. The situation in Ireland became so confused that Pius had to issue a decree in August 1460 appointing Fr Nehemias as Irish Observant Vicar Provincial. This decree may be taken as the point at which the Irish Observants attained maturity. From 1460 until 1517 the Irish Province was ruled by a Conventual Minister Provincial and an Observant Vicar Provincial. The Province, like the Order, split into two in 1517.

The official recognition of the Observants in Ireland in 1460 gave a new impetus to expansion. Within a year, the reformers had taken over the old friaries at Youghal, Timoleague and Multyfarnham. They soon moved into those parts of Ireland which had never been touched by English influence, with new foundations at such sites as Sherkin, Bantry, Kilcrea, Lislaughlin, Donegal and Dromahair. The Conventuals also tried to expand into these areas, with foundations in such places as Monaghan, Galbally, Stradbally and Aran. This was also a period of great architectural vitality. In addition to new buildings, many old friaries were enlarged by the addition of chapels or renovated with new windows etc. The most beautiful of Franciscan ruins today date from this period, e.g. Moyne, Lislaughlin, Kilconnell, Adare and especially Dromahair.

The two parts of the Province lived in reasonable harmony. As the number of friars varied, a friary occasionally changed its loyalty from one part of the Province to the other. Sometimes this was due to the influence of the local chief, as when the Observants of Donegal took over Carrickfergus in 1497. In this period, the Irish Province attained its maximum size of about sixty guardianates. A reasonable guess would put the total number of friars at around six hundred.

Later history of the Irish Conventuals

When Pope Leo X split the Order into two by the Bull *Ite et Vos* of the 29th. May 1517, Fr Philip Ó Maighreáin became the first Irish Observant Provincial. We do not know the name of the corresponding Conventual Provincial. The two Irish Provinces remained on good terms, although there were occasional disputes about which friary belonged to whom (e.g. Galway and Armagh in 1533).

Since the Conventuals generally had richer houses situated in areas under English control, they bore the full brunt of the initial suppression of the monasteries under Henry VIII. At this time, some twenty-two friaries remained under the Conventual Provincial. Many of these houses seem to have been understaffed. Since most of these friaries were in areas where tight English control was possible, the communities were rapidly dispersed. In exceptional circumstances, some friars were killed. Most were able to live on with help from the local people. A few joined up with the Observant friars. When the Conventual community at Monaghan was dispersed by an English army in 1540, Fr Raymond MacMahon went to live with the Observant community at Multyfarnham, where he died many years later with a reputation for sanctity.

With the break-up of the community life, it proved impossible to train new friars. Eventually the Irish Conventual Province ceased to exist as an independent unit. At least from 1556, it and Scotland were governed by an appointed Commissary General. Through the influence of Shane O'Neill, the Irish Conventuals did get permission to elect a Provincial in 1564, but in December of that same year an Italian, Jerome Fiorati, was appointed to the post. The remaining Conventuals seem to have joined the Observants as a body, probably in 1566. They remained near their old friaries. When the English raided Roscrea in 1579, they captured two Conventuals. Fr Tadhg O'Daly was killed when he refused to apostatize. The other friar was released when he gave in to this request. When Fr Donagh Mooney ofm. gave a mission in the area in 1611, the ex-friar repented, was re-admitted to the friars and led a life of penitence for his sin.

By 1600, the Conventual Franciscans had, for all practical purposes, ceased to exist in Ireland. The reason for their downfall seems twofold. Their style of life seems to have made them timid, so that they lacked the will to survive. Secondly their connections with the English areas in Ireland made them easy targets for the authorities.

Fr Maurice O'Fihely

The brightest star of the Irish Conventuals was the theologian Fr Maurice O'Fihely. He joined the friars about 1475 and studied at Oxford. He first emerged into prominence in 1488 when he was regent of studies at the Franciscan College in Milan. He obtained a similar post at Padua in 1491 and became a leading member of the Scotistic school there. This interest was probably based on a mistaken belief that John Duns Scotus was an Irishman. Fr Maurice, or *Flos Mundi* (The Flower of the World) as he was known to his contemporaries, prepared a four-volume edition of Scotus, which was printed in Venice in 1506. He also published commentaries on the works of Scotus. He was an influential figure at the General Chapter of the Conventuals in 1506. That same year he was appointed Archbishop of Tuam. In this capacity, he attended the Fifth Lateran Council in 1512. Soon after, he began his return journey to Ireland, but died in Galway on 24th. June 1513 before reaching Tuam. On this note we may leave the Irish Conventuals.

Dromahair Friary: Finial

23

Chapter 4

THE OBSERVANTS AND THE SUPPRESSION
(1536 — 1615)

In the last chapter, we traced the history of the Irish Conventual Franciscans up to their extinction about 1600. The rest of our history concerns the Observants. Following the division of the Order in 1517, they continued to expand. They built the last medieval Irish Franciscan friary at Creevelea, beside Dromahair, Co. Leitrim. Built in the flamboyant style typical of the Irish revival of the period, I consider it the most beautiful of all the medieval Franciscan sites in Ireland.

By this time, Henry VIII had come to the English throne and had begun his new religious policies. The Reformation in Ireland is a much more complex topic than most people believe. In its early stages, we may best consider it as an extension of English law and custom to Ireland. This is also the case with the Suppression of the Irish Monasteries. Abbeys generally had become quite rich by this period. Communities were small. There was a flourishing trade in sub-letting monastic properties. We can think of the first stages of the Suppression as the nationalisation of these resources by the king and their transfer to his favoured friends. In contrast to the abbeys, friaries were generally small. They were not very rich and had vigorous communities. They were only caught up in the initial suppression because the legal mind did not like an unfinished job and because many minor leaders wanted to share in every possible piece of the loot.

The initial stages of the Suppression

The Irish 'Act of Supremacy' and the first legislation about the monasteries were introduced in the parliament of 1536, a number of years later than their English equivalents. The Supremacy legislation was passed in May without any difficulty. Parliament dragged its feet over the Suppression Bill, which was not passed until October 1537. This delay had less to do with religion than with practical politics and patronage resulting from the appointment of Lord Grey as Deputy. In fact the Suppression had already begun, but only of a few large abbeys within the Pale.

George Brown, an ex-Augustinian, had become Archbishop of Dublin in 1536. Late in 1537 he started a campaign to administer the oath of Supremacy and to persuade the friars to preach royal supremacy. While many took the oath, they did not bother about its implications. A campaign of passive resistance started. Brown then attempted to absorb the Observant friars within Conventual communities. This policy had been quite successful in England, where the Observants were small in number. It could not work in Ireland, where they were both numerous and active. Upset by his failure to deal with the Observants in this way, it would seem that Brown proceeded to suppress the Franciscan houses in Dublin and at Kilcullen in the spring of 1539. By autumn the campaign had spread to all parts of Ireland which were under English influence. By the end of 1540, most of the friaries in the more accessible areas had been suppressed. Generally these houses yielded little to the royal funds. The buildings were handed over to new masters. The communities were dispersed. However there was no real pressure to conform until the reign of Edward VI.

One of the first to preach publicly against the new laws was Dr Saul ofm., in Waterford on 1st. Sunday of Lent, 10th. March 1538. His words earned him a cell in Dublin Castle. A report by a private agent, Thomas Agard, to Thomas Cromwell on 5th. April 1538 reveals the the Observant element in all Orders, including the Franciscans, were aware of the trend of events:— 'So that here (in Ireland) the blood of Christ is clean blotted out of all men's hearts (i.e. the blood of the Reform), what with that monster, the Observants, as they will be called most holiest, so that there remains more virtue in one of their coats and knotted girdles than ever was in Christ and His Passion'. In 1540, the Vicar Provincial of the Franciscan Observants rushed to Rome, warning all the authorities on his route as to what was happening. At the same time, the more unscrupulous of the laity began to reap the financial benefits of Suppression. This was especially true since it was the policy of the new Lord Deputy, St Leger, to 'kill Rome's rule by kindness'. Initial efforts to introduce the Counter-Reform to the country through political means, such as the Geraldine League, failed. The Irish remained Catholic, but in the pre-Reformation medieval tradition. It took many years before Counter-Reformation catholicism became the norm in Ireland.

Archbishop Myler Magrath

To high-light the confusion of the times in religious matters, we may take the career of the famous Franciscan Archbishop of Cashel, Myler Magrath. He was born about 1522 as a member of an Irish princely family. He seems to have joined the Conventual friars at Downpatrick, and studied for a while on the Continent. Soon after his return to Ireland, he was sent to Rome for the purpose of obtaining the See of Down and Connor for one of the young O'Neills. He turned out to be such a good diplomat, that he obtained the see for himself in Oct. 1565, yet retained the friendship of the O'Neills!

25

Soon after this, he judged the way the wind was blowing and he submitted to Queen Elizabeth at Drogheda on 31st. May 1567. In return he received confirmation in his see, but as an Anglican prelate. He added Clogher to Down and Connor in 1570, and Cashel and Emly in the following year. He was unfortunate in that his first wife died early in marriage, but he latter married Annie O'Meara. By pleading his poverty, he added the dioceses of Waterford and Lismore to his collection in 1580 and those of Killala and Achonry in 1607.

All this does not mean that he was a dyed-in-the-wool Protestant. He was extremely avaricious, proud and a real politician. Thus he arrested a number of friars for preaching against the Queen in 1571, but he rapidly released them when James FitzMaurice FitzGerald threatened to burn his property. Even his persecution of Catholics was two-edged. If such were possible, he must have been embarrassed in 1582 when a letter of his from London was seized and found to contain warnings to certain Catholic bishops and priests of their imminent arrest. With Myler's active co-operation, his wife warned many priests of intended raids.

He was declared a notorious heretic when the Holy See deprived him of the see of Down and Connor in 1580. He entered into frequent and very secret negotiations with several friars with the intention of reverting to Catholicism. The greatest secret of his life is whether he was received back into the Catholic Church before his death in December 1622 at the reputed age of a hundred Yet his whole career shows that it is extremely difficult to judge the religious patterns of the men of his age.

Catholic relief under Queen Mary

After the death of King Edward VI, the friars breathed a sigh of relief. With no permanent houses, it had become almost impossible to train young novices. The Franciscans hoped for a lull in the persecution when the Catholic Queen Mary came to the throne. Two friars went to London in 1554 to request the return of Multyfarnham (where the friars were still living), Carrickfergus, Enniscorthy, Kilcullen and Trim. Much though she would like to have granted their request, political and financial conditions dictated that Mary could not do so. The friars continued to live in small communities, occasionally using their old buildings, when local leaders were sympathetic. Franciscans in other countries were willing to help. Thus individual friars were frequently living on the Continent, where they could study and work in peace.

Persecution under Queen Elizabeth I

Queen Elizabeth I came to the throne in 1558. Initially, nothing changed, except perhaps that a few of the larger communities had to disperse. Trouble arose following the foundation of the Desmond Confederation in 1569. This started a long series of minor wars during which armies swept the land. Foreign aid was sought and sent in the classic political gambit of the period: Catholic princes were willing to send help to re-conquer the country for the Catholic religion. This was an extension of the principle 'cuius regio, eius religio', (the religion of a country was that of its ruler). The Irish Franciscans living on the Continent were deeply involved. Examples would be Fr Seán O'Farrell, who was hanged at Askeaton in 1587, and Fr James O'Shea, who carried the Papal Banner ashore when the Spanish landed near Dingle in July 1579. The rise of the Desmond Confederation coincided with the final excommunication of Elizabeth by Pope Pius V in 1570. From then on, the battle between Catholicism and the English authorities became more intense.

A period of almost systematic persecution began. Any friar who had the misfortune to be captured by the British armies on the march was put to death. By the time Queen Elizabeth died, the list of friars known to have been killed had grown to about thirty five. It included such men as Rory MacCongail who, after various escapes, was flogged to death at Armagh possibly as early as 1565; Fergal Ward, the Guardian of Armagh, was hanged there in 1575; Fr Donal O'Neillan was thrown a number of times from the top of Trinity Gate, Youghal, and then used for target practice, in 1585; three friars were captured and killed at Downpatrick in 1575; an old friar, Felim O'Hara, was killed before the altar at Moyne because he would not reveal the hiding place of the sacred vessels; Fr John O'Dowd, also of Moyne, was killed in 1579 for not revealing confessional secrets.

Dr Patrick O'Healy

A typical friar of the period would be Dr Patrick O'Healy. He joined the friars at Dromahair and studied first at Alcalá in Spain and later at Aracoeli in Rome. Appointed Bishop of Mayo in July 1576, his plans to return to Ireland were upset and he became the Roman agent for FitzMaurice and the Desmond Confederation. On his way to Ireland, he stayed in Paris for a while and his learning created quite an impression. He was joined by Conn O'Rourke ofm. — one of the O'Rourkes of Breffny. They slipped ashore, probably in North Kerry, during the summer of 1579. It seems that Dr O'Healy carried plans for an intended Spanish invasion. They made their way to the Desmond castle at Askeaton. In the Earl's absence, his wife received them well, but also warned the Mayor of Limerick of their presence. When they resumed their journey, they were arrested and taken, first to Limerick, then to Kilmallock. There they were questioned about the invasion plans and tortured by flogging and also by nailing through the hands. In addition, the authorities demanded that they recognise Elizabeth as Head of the Irish Church. This they refused to do. They were condemned immediately by the Lord Deputy, Sir William Drury. Both were hanged and their bodies used for target practice.

The Counter-Reformation

Much of the attitude of those times seems strange to us. We find it hard to understand the bloody behaviour of armies, and the intertwining of politics and religion. This is the period when faith and fatherland began to be associated in the sense in which we have understood them in Ireland since. Yet even the Catholic church in Ireland in those days was undergoing a reform. Priests trained in the Counter-Reformation tradition on the Continent brought the theology of the Council of Trent to Ireland and the traditions of the Celtic church were slowly replaced.

The new friars returning to Ireland were also men of the Counter-Reformation. The plantations in Munster, begun by Catholic Queen Mary, made life difficult in the south of Ireland for the friars. They continued to flourish under Irish protection in the north. About five old friaries remained in action, but there were places of refuge all over the country. A new foundation was made at Lisgoole, near Lough Erne. Training was difficult, but the Continental education was excellent. Numbers were low and morale was sagging among the friars when Elizabeth died in 1603. Irish life and culture was fading after Kinsale and the Flight of the Earls. Yet faced with all these difficulties, the Irish friars replied with a fresh outburst of zeal and energy.

Chapter 5
THE GOLDEN AGE OF THE IRISH FRANCISCANS (1615 — 1697)

'The history of the Irish Franciscans during the seventeenth century is more glorious than that of any other province'— thus Fr Lucian Ceyssens ofm., an expert on that period. After the persecution of the Elizabethan era and following the defeat of Irish nobility at Kinsale, one would expect the Irish Franciscans to be in poor shape at the start of the seventeenth century. Despite all this, they rebounded with renewed energy and became a powerful force engaged in gathering the remnants of Irish culture and in preaching the new theology of the Counter-Reformation.

The dynamic leadership of Fr Donagh Mooney

Catholic Ireland had hoped that the coronation of the first of the Stuarts, James I, would bring a period of rest. It brought further persecution as the Viceroy, Lord Mountjoy, tried to extend English rule throughout the country. When the Irish Provincial Chapter met in 1612, only the friaries of Donegal, Armagh and Multyfarnham had regular communities. The number of guardians in the Province was reduced to eight. A Westmeath-man, Fr Donagh Mooney, continued in office as Vicar Provincial. It was decided that the novices would be trained on the Continent at the new foundation in Louvain.

At the next Chapter, held in Waterford on 18th. September 1615, Donagh Mooney was elected Provincial by unanimous vote. This man of boundless energy was about to get Franciscan life rejuvenated in Ireland once again, helped by such men as Florence Conry and Luke Wadding. The Chapter issued statutes on many matters. Preaching was re-organised, and a strict examination for faculties was introduced. Eight friars were admitted to the Irish Province from other provinces while six were expelled.

Fr Donagh Mooney was born near Ballymore about 1577 and joined the Franciscans, possibly following a military career, at Donegal early in October 1600. Before he could finish his novitiate, Donegal friary was destroyed and he was transferred to Multyfarnham. Two days before his profession, the Irish Provincial, Fr John McGrath, was captured with some other friars. In order to make his profession Br Donagh Mooney let himself be captured and took his Franciscan vows imprisoned in the same cell with the Minister Provincial! He escaped in a matter of days and acted as guardian of Armagh at a Chapter held in woods near Leitrim. Ordained at Dromahair, he went to France to complete his studies and was soon appointed the first guardian of the new college at Louvain in Belgium during 1606-7. On his return to Ireland he was stationed in Drogheda. He became second-in-command of the Irish Franciscans and was elected Provincial in 1615. He wrote an account of his visitation of all friaries in Ireland, probably at Louvain on his way to the General Chapter of the Order at Salamanca in 1618. He added some historical notes later and the result, the *Tractatus de Provincia Hiberniae*, is a major source for Irish Franciscan history. Donagh Mooney died at Drogheda in April 1624. During his term of office, small residences were established at Cavan, Clonmel, Dublin, Kilnalahan, Limerick, Lisgoole, New Ross and Wexford. By the end of his period as Provincial, there were some one hundred and twenty friars in Ireland (of whom thirty-three were approved preachers), a start had been made on a permanent building in Louvain and this college had already sent about twenty five well-trained priests back to Ireland.

The mission to Scotland

As the morale of the Franciscans in Ireland improved, they were able and willing to consider helping their Celtic brethren in Scotland. Fr John Ogilvie, a Scottish friar who had been living in the new college at Louvain, not to be confused with his Jesuit name-sake, returned to Scotland in 1612. The next year he was joined by a Scottish brother, John Stuart, who had the vital local knowledge and who knew Scots Gaelic. Since the Protestant ministers could not speak Gaelic, many of the people were still Catholic but had not seen a priest for nearly fifty years. Br John travelled back and forth to Louvain, where he died in 1625. He supplied fresh information about the mission and encouraged more priests to go there. Financial problems delayed the departure of Frs Patrick Brady for the Highlands and Edmund McCann for the Hebridies until 4th. Jan. 1619. Fr Edmund was arrested and banished. He returned with the next group of priests: Frs Paul O'Neill, Patrick Hegarty and Cornelius Ward. The abandoned Third Order Friary at Bonamargy in North Antrim was taken over as a base. Lack of funds and the political situation forced the closure of the mission in 1637. Fr Patrick Hegary remained at Bonamargy until his death in 1637. Many people came across the North Channel for his spiritual services. Four missionaries were selected to re-open the mission, but they could not travel. Efforts to re-open the mission in 1647-8 also failed, but the friars did return before the end of the century. There were six working in the area in 1699 and five in 1703. This dropped to two in 1730. These must have left within a few years, since two friars could not be found to go to Scotland in 1766.

The Continental Colleges

An obvious solution to the problem of training young Franciscans for work in Ireland was the opening of houses in Catholic countries on the Continent. Individual friars had been educated outside Ireland for a number of years. The obvious choice for the site of the first Irish Franciscan Continental College was *Louvain* (now officially Leuven) in Belgium. On a well-known trade route, it was the site of a famous university and was in a country governed by militantly Catholic Spain. The College of St Anthony was founded there in 1606, and moved to its present site in 1617. Fr Luke Wadding, again with some Spanish help, founded St Isidore's College in *Rome*. Most of the first community arrived from Louvain on 21st. June 1625. Fr Malachy Fallon was sent eastwards from Louvain in 1629 to seek another foundation. His mission resulted in the College of the Immaculate Conception at *Prague* which was officially opened on 6th. July 1631. Sympathetic Polish friars gave the Irish a loan of a friary at *Wielun* for a number of years. Further efforts produced a temporary residence at *Paris*, but foundations at Jablonow (Poland) and Namslav (Silesia) were unsuccessful. From Rome, a novitiate was opened at *Capranica* in 1656.

These colleges, and the later foundation at *Boulay*, provided a steady flow of priests until most of them were closed about the time of the French Revolution. On average, about ten friars returned from the Continent each year. Prague, with a capacity of up to a hundred friars, provided five or six; Louvain had a capacity of about forty and provided two or three new priests each year; Rome was similar to Louvain. Clerical training was fairly strict: a year's novitiate in Ireland or on the Continent, followed by four years of philosophy and theology on the Continent during which there was constant training in preaching and casuistry in both Irish and English, and ending with exams on returning to Ireland. Initially discipline in the colleges was quite strict, although abuses did creep in at a later stage. Without these colleges, the Irish friars would have ceased to exist.

Ireland within the German Belgian Nation

The structure of the Franciscan Order on the Continent had been re-organised during the sixteenth century. About 1526 the office of Commissary of the German-Belgian Nation was created. The Commissary had authority over most of the provinces in Germany, those in Belgium and also those in England and Ireland. It is hard to discover when he began to exercise his authority over the Irish friars. His role was already obvious at the time of the foundation of St Anthony's College, Louvain, in 1606.

31

In 1633 General Statutes were approved by which the General Constitutions adopted at the General Chapter at Segovia in 1621 were adapted to the needs of the German-Belgian Nation. These Statutes remained the basic law for the Irish Franciscans down to the end of the nineteenth century. The standard interpretation used was that of a Belgian friar named Kerchove.

Some time in the mid-seventeenth century, the Irish Province took the name Recollect. This title, and membership of the German-Belgian Nation, were of little practical importance in the life of the Irish friars, except for a brief period in the mid-nineteenth century.

Steady progress from Fr Donagh Mooney to 1640

After the period in office of Fr Donagh Mooney, the friars continued their quiet work in a spirit of hope. The Archbishop of Dublin reported to Rome in 1623: '. . . to these must be added about two hundred Franciscans, who are especially to be commended, because they never suffered themselves to become extinct in the kingdom, and were the only religious who maintained the fight in some districts . . . ' While there had been many arrests during the early part of the century, few of those imprisoned were put to death. One of the exceptions was Dr Cornelius O'Devany ofm., Bishop of Down and Connor, who was hanged at Dublin in 1612.

A Provincial Chapter was held in Limerick in 1629 and it is the first for which the full Chapter Bill is extant. It nearly ended in disaster when the drunken behaviour of some of the 'hangers-on' attracted the attention of the city authorities. While there had been only eight guardianates in 1612, superiors could now be appointed to houses in: Limerick, Cork, Quin, Sherkin, Timoleague, Kilcrea, Youghal, Cashel, Clonmel, Waterford, New Ross, Wexford, Kilkenny, Kildare, Dublin, Multyfarnham, Athlone, Drogheda, Cavan, Dundalk, Lisgoole, Armagh, Carrickfergus, Down, Donegal, Dromahair, Moyne, Ross, Kilnalahan, Galway, Kilconnell and Trim. Special arrangements were made for Muckross and Lislaughlin. Appointments were also made for the Continental colleges, but this had to be done in a rather complicated manner. Twenty five houses were listed as vacant. This Chapter showed the steady progress which had been made. It was followed by one of those periods of mild persecution typical of the century and usually coinciding with a change of viceroy. However this only slightly retarded the expansion of the friars during these years.

Provincialism

At this time it begins to become obvious that one's civil province of origin was important. Each of the Continental colleges became

32

associated to a limited extent with friars from one area: Prague for the Leinstermen, Louvain for the Ulstermen & Connaughtmen, Rome for the Munstermen, Paris for the Anglo-Irish. Each of the four definitors (the assistants to the Provincial) had to be from a different province. The Provincial also came from each province in turn. These practices as regards Provincial and definitors continued down to the middle of the nineteenth century.

About 1623 an effort was made to split the Irish Province into two on a racial basis: Munster-Leinster (for the Anglo-Irish) and Ulster-Connacht (for the Old Irish). The Provincial Chapter at Athlone in 1644 requested a formal division into two provinces. This was approved by the General Chapter at Toledo in 1645, but was rejected by the Provincial Chapter at Ross in 1647. Except for a brief resurrection at the Chapter at Buttevant in 1673, the matter was allowed to die quietly. The spirit of provincialism remained alive. Thus an Italian friar, Visitator of the Irish Province, could say that the Provincial, outside his civil province of origin, was like a foreigner in another country (un Provinciale forastiero di lontan paese).

The Confederation of Kilkenny

Expansion had continued during the 1630's and the friars were in a very strong position when war broke out in 1641. There were communities in forty seven houses (ten still vacant). There was a strong Continental system of support. There were some six hundred members in the Province. The strongly Catholic athmosphere of the times encouraged further expansion. New foundations were made in such unpromising places as Jamestown in Protestant mid-Leitrim and Ballinabarny in desolate South Wicklow. Some neglected Third Order foundations were revived as First Order houses — Ballinasaggart, Ballymote, Killeenagallive, possibly Killedan/Mons Pietatis. By 1646, there was a total of sixty two communities.

The friars on the Continent became involved politically in the affairs of the Confederation. Thus Fr Francis O'Sullivan arranged for the transport of supplies from Spain, Fr James FitzSimons acted as a secret agent in London and Fr Luke Wadding was a major Irish agent in Rome.

Just as the politicians in the Confederation were split over their basic loyalties, so also the friars were split over loyalty to Rinuccini, the Papal Nuncio, or to Ormond, the politician. The majority of the friars remained faithful to the Nuncio, possibly remembering the part played by Luke Wadding in bringing him to Ireland. The Provincial Chapter of 1648 had to be held under the protection of Owen Roe O'Neill, since the Ormondists wished to halt it. The bitter infighting

33

between the friars rapidly faded with the arrival of Oliver Cromwell at Dublin in 1649. Significantly, the semi-national synod which condemned Ormond in 1650 was held in the friary at Jamestown. The split within the friars, which reflected the national split between Irish and Anglo-Irish, was papered over until the Restoration.

Persecution under Cromwell

The friars suffered heavily under Cromwell. Within a year of his arrival about ten friars had been killed, including the Franciscan Bishop of Elphin, Dr Boetius Egan. He had been captured by troops involved in the siege of Clonmel and was hanged and dismembered near Macroom. In 1651 about another ten friars were killed. Details are hard to discover, since the friars rapidly went underground and ceased to keep records. In so far as they were able, they continued to minister in the areas around the old friaries, but the buildings themselves were often taken over by the Cromwellian authorities. Individual friars were pursued relentlessly and killed when caught: e.g. Fr Eugene O'Cahan, a well-known lecturer of philosophy and theology during his years in Italy, was captured in North Kerry, released, re-captured in North Cork and killed in 1652; Fr John Kearney was hanged in Clonmel jail on 20th. March 1652.

On 6th. Jan. 1653 the Commissioners of the English Parliament for Irish affairs issued an edict banishing all 'persons in Popish Orders' and even provided ships for those who wished to go. With over forty friars dead, some of those remaining in the country chose exile. A number went to the Continental Colleges, but many settled wherever they arrived. When Fr Isaac Horan ofm. was returning to Louvain with the remains of Dr Florence Conry, the founder of St Anthony's College, he met three Irish friars in a tiny fishing village in Castille in the autumn of 1653. Many priests became chaplains to Irish regiments etc. — there were eight of them with the Spanish army in Flanders in 1654. A few settled in other Franciscan provinces and the Minister General had to issue regulations to force them to correspond in civilised Latin. They had been writing letters in Irish and the continentals were suspicious of what might be happening.

Many friars remained in Ireland. Fr John Dalton ofm. was the only priest in Kilkenny at the time of his capture on the Feast of the Portiuncula in 1653. Hanged and quartered on 5th. Aug., he was the last friar to fall victim to the Cromwellians. Five pounds remained the reward for information about a priest. Two camps were set up, one on Aran, the other on Inishboffin Island, to house priests. Transportation, particularly to the Barbadoes, was quite common. Despite all this, the friars continued their work in many different parts of the country.

34

By 1658 things were sufficiently quiet to enable the friars to hold a Provincial Chapter at Ballinasaggart. Fr Bernard Egan was elected Provincial, but such was the uncertainty of the times that four others were nominated to succeed him, if necessary. Superiors were appointed for some thirty friaries, mainly in the Midlands, the West and the North East. By 1661 all friaries seem to have been restored. There was an estimated total of two hundred friars in Ireland and one hundred and fifty on the Continent. The friars were aided in their work by the extensive faculties granted them by Paul V in 1612 and again by Alexander VII in 1655.

The Restoration: a troubled period

The early years of King Charles II were difficult ones for the Catholic church in Ireland. It took some time for the hierarchy to be re-vitalised. Unsavoury rows broke out between priests and religious over rights. One of the most infamous of these was between the Franciscans and the Dominicans in Ulster in which St Oliver Plunkett played a major role. The basic problem behind all these difficulties was a lack of money to support the clergy properly.

Perhaps the most unsavoury item for the Franciscans was the re-emergence of the Nuncio/Ormond split in the activities of Fr Peter Walsh ofm. His activities are best summed up in the phrase 'An Irish Gallican Interlude', since the point at issue was civil control of church affairs. The Restoration of Charles II in May 1660 had raised Catholic hopes. Fr Peter was appointed Irish Catholic agent in London in Jan. 1661. The previous month some laymen in Dublin, mainly Anglo-Irish, had drafted a formula of loyalty which contained a statement of grievances, a petition for protection, and a protestation of allegiance (afterwards known as the Remonstrance). With the help of Ormond (now Lord Lieutenant), Fr Peter began to seek support for the formula in Ireland by all the means at his disposal. Eventually Ormond arranged a national synod for Dublin in June 1666. Even this special synod would only accept a modified version of the formula. Ormond then tried to get the Franciscan Order to accept it, since the friars were meeting in Provincial Chapter. Complete confusion reigned and the Chapter had to be adjourned. Fr Peter fought on, writing much in defence of his own viewpoint. Although excommunicated in 1670, he submitted shortly before his death in 1688.

Another famous Franciscan of the same period was Fr James Taaffe ofm., appointed visitator of Ireland by the papal authorities in 1666. The exact terms of his appointment are rather nebulous, but it seems that he was not granted the special faculties which he considered necessary. On his arrival in Ireland in March 1668 after a delay of two years, he claimed the title of apostolic visitator and commissary general of the Irish Church. He tried to untangle the undergrowth of church jurisdiction, by then a veritable jungle following nearly fifteen years without episcopal supervision. His decisions were generally so unpopular that nearly all of them were appealed to Rome. In 1671 Fr Taaffe himself arrived back in Rome, was fully absolved from all censures and the whole incident was quietly forgotten.

The activities of Taaffe and Walsh delayed the re-organisation of the Irish friars. Rome appointed Fr Peter Gaynor as Vicar Provincial in 1669. He was able to appoint supperiors to fifty six friaries, leaving seven vacant. A full normal Chapter was held at Elphin in 1672. By then there were sufficient friars in Ireland to appoint superiors for all the houses in the country. Re-organisation continued even during the periods of mild persecution in 1673-74 and again during the Titus Oates plot in 1678.

The Ven. Charles Meehan

St Oliver Plunkett is the best-known Irish victim of the Titus Oates plot. The first priest arrested, and in a sense the most unfortunate, was the Irish Franciscan, Fr Charles Meehan. His cause is being actively promoted in England at the moment. It was formally introduced in 1886. Fr Charles Meehan was ordained in Ireland without having done systematic studies. He fled to the Continent in 1673-74, studied in Bavaria and Rome, and began his homeward trip to Ireland. He was shipwrecked off Wales while trying to return to his native country. Being a stranger with documents from the Continent, he was automatically arrested. Like some other priests just before this, he would normally have been released after a couple of months. Unfortunately the Titus Oates plot had just become public. Imprisoned at Denbigh in North Wales, he was an embarrassment to the people, since they had to pay the costs of his detention. They asked London for permission to release him, but this was refused. On orders from London, he was tried at Ruthin and condemned for being a Catholic priest. He was put to death at Denbigh on 12th. Aug. 1679.

Literary activities

The Golden Age of the Irish Franciscans is mainly associated with their tremendous literary output. Initially this came from Louvain with a heavy emphasis on Irish culture, but gradually the writings of the Irish friars at Rome and Prague became prominent, with the stress on Franciscanism and on theology.

The Louvain school is best known for the activities of Br Michael O'Cleary, compiler, with Fearfeasa Ó Maolconaire, Cúcoigcríche Ó Duibhgennáin and Cúcoigcríche O'Cleary, of the *Annals of the Four Masters*. Completed in 1637, it was not printed until 1851. As a result of his work and that of other friars of the Louvain school, there is still a huge collection of Irish manuscripts in Brussels. He also wrote *Focloir, nó Sanasan Nua*, as well as helping in the compilation of the *Réim ríoghraidhe na hÉireann agus senchas a naomh*.

The first known Irish grammar, *Rudimenta grammaticae hibernicae*, and the first Irish Catechism, which was also the first book printed in an Irish fount, *Teagasc Críosdaidhe*, (Antwerp 1611, later reprinted at Louvain and in Rome), were the work of Fr Bonaventure O'Hussey. The catechism was one of a number of books produced in Louvain in order to educate Irish catholics in good counter-reformation theology. As one friar wrote: 'nach do mhúnadh Gaoidhilge sgriobhmaoid ach do mhúnadh na haithridhe'. Other examples would be: Florence Conry's *Desiderius*; Antoine Gearon's *Parrthas an Anma*; Aodh MacAingil's *Scáthán Shacramuinte na hAithridhe*.

Fr Florence Conry, the founder of St Anthony's College in Louvain, had studied St Augustine and was a friend of Cornelius Jansens, with whom he engaged in theological dialogue. As such he was much respected by the early Jansenists. Examples of his works would be: *Doctrine of Grace according to St Augustine*, *Tractatus de statu parvulorum*, and *Tractatus de Augustini sensu . . . B.V.M. Conceptionem*. Notes made by Fr Luke Wadding in Rome are also a major source for the history of Jansenism.

In Rome Fr Luke Wadding prepared an edition of the writings of St Francis. His main effort went into organising the monumental *Annales Ordinis Minorum* — envisaged as a gigantic history of the Franciscans — and the *Scriptores Ordinis Minorum* — a complete list of Franciscan authors. Wadding was also the inspiration behind the first critical edition of Duns Scotus (Lyons, 1639 ss.), although most of the work was done by John Punch, Anthony Hickey and Aodh MacAingil.

Other important Irish Franciscan works of the period include: Francis Molloy's *Lucerna fidelium* — another Irish catechism; the work of Fr John Colgan on the lives of the Irish saints — *Triadis Thaumaturgae, & Acta Sanctorum I*; the summary histories of the Irish Franciscans prepared by Fr Donagh Mooney and also by Fr Francis Matthews; the works of Fr Maurice Conry and also of Fr Anthony Broudin on the lives of the Irish martyrs. The complete edition of the works of **Fr Bonaventure Baron** came to twenty two volumes. Individual works would include the *Collectanea sacra* of Fr **Patrick Fleming**; the *Summa theologica* of Francis Bermingham; the *Roma triumphans septicollis* of Raymond Caron.

This is just a small selection of the material which made the seventeenth century the Golden Age of the Irish Franciscans.

Kilkenny Friary: Irish King

Chapter 6

THE EIGHTEENTH CENTURY: SLOW DECLINE (1696 — 1782)

Following the coronation of James II in 1685, the friars expected greater toleration for the catholic religion. The Provincial Chapter at Ross in 1687 appointed superiors to fifty six houses in Ireland. Most of these were staffed by friars trained in the continental colleges. After the Battle of the Boyne, it would seem that King Billy was willing to treat Catholics with toleration. However English politics and politicians dictated otherwise. 1697 was a critical year for religious in Ireland, since it saw the passing of the 'Banishment of Religious Act'. Hopes that the royal assent would be refused proved delusory, and the Act came into force in May 1698. Meeting in Dublin on the 15th. Feb., the Provincial Definitory had decided to obey the Act in principle. Goods would be given into safe keeping, novices sent to the continent, while permission would be sought for the old and infirm friars to remain in Ireland. Two years later, in 1700, we have the first set of reliable statistics for the Irish Franciscans: four hundred and twenty priests, fifty four brothers, nineteen students and sixteen novices — a total of five hundred and nine friars. The direct and indirect effects of persecution would reduce this total to about one hundred and fifty friars by 1782.

The friars outside Ireland

Many friars obeyed the Act of Banishment by going to live on the Continent. With the help of the Duke of Lorraine, a new college was founded at Boulay, near Metz, in 1698. The following year the Pope was reputedly helping to support two hundred and fourteen Irish friars in French territory. However, many of the friars settled in their own Irish continental colleges. A number obtained posts as military chaplains with various armies. Thus Fr Charles Fleming ofm. was accidentally shot by a firing-squad while absolving a deserter at Gravelines in 1739; Fr John Clarke ofm. was reputedly with the Irish at Fontenoy in 1745; Fr Bonaventure O'Donoghue was with the French army in Louisiana in 1718. Many friars sailed the seas as naval chaplains. Some became chaplains to the nobility, e.g. Fr Bernard Kelly ofm., chaplain and secretary to the Young Pretender. Finally a number of friars found refuge in other provinces of the Order: e.g. Fr Sylvester Lloyd, afterwards bishop of Killaloe and later of Waterford, lived with the English Franciscans at Douai, where he edited an Irish catechism.

The friars who remained in Ireland

The Franciscans who decided to remain in Ireland rather than obey the Act of Banishment found that the application of the new Act was rather spasmodic. Conditions deteriorated from 1705 on. There were arrests, and a few religious died in gaol from ill-health and neglect. The friars lived in relative peace in small cottages or houses. From about 1710 on small communities began to form once again.

One method of evading the law was to register as diocesan priests, since the persecution was directed more against bishops and religious than against the parochial clergy. As early as 1714, the Provincial Chapter had to lay down rules for friars acting as diocesan clergy. Many Franciscans took charge of parishes near their old friaries. Others took over large areas, especially in South Ulster and the Midlands, where they carried on a wide pastoral activity. Thus the friars at Multyfarnham served that parish while living in a small cottage from about 1705 up to 1824. The friars of Trim served a huge area around Courtown from about 1720 to 1826. The friars of Monaghan town moved out into a very large area of South Monaghan. While the friars moved into parish work in a number of the larger towns, an unusual system evolved in Wexford, Waterford and Clonmel by which they helped the parochial clergy by working in the parish church while living in their own house.

Gradually the friars came out into the open, often with the connivance of the local authorities. From about 1723 on, the Galway friars were saying mass in public, yet the mayor never found anyone on the premises whenever he raided their house!

Due to their Continental training, and also Franciscan influence at the court-in-exile of the Stuarts at St Germain, many friars were appointed bishops in Ireland. In Killala: Dr Tady Francis O'Rourke (1707-36), Dr Peter Archdeken (1736-39), Dr Bonaventure McDonnell (1749-60). In Dromore: Dr Denis Maguire (1767-70), who was translated to Kilmore (1770-93), Dr Patrick Brady (1770-80). In Down and Connor: Dr James O'Shiel (1717-24), Dr Francis Stuart (1740-51). In Ferns: Dr Ambrose O'Callaghan (1729-44). In Killaloe: Dr Sylvester Lloyd (1729-39), who was translated to Waterford and Lismore (1739-47).

The novitiate question and the Roman reaction

In an effort to maintain their numbers, the friars began to admit novices in various houses even though the canonical requirements for a novitiate could not be completely fulfilled. It became customary to ordain candidates to the priesthood before they began their studies. Such young men could proceed to one of the colleges on the

Continent and support themselves, at least partially, by accepting stipends for masses and other services. The bishops used a similar system to train Irish diocesan priests.

This practice was open to obvious abuses and eventually Rome decided to act. Fr John Kent (President of the Irish Pastoral College at Louvain) was sent to investigate in 1742. For the diocesan clergy, it was eventually decided to impose the obligation of residence on the bishops and to limit the number of priests they might ordain. For religious in general, and the friars in particular, a set of Decrees was promulgated by Propaganda Fide in Rome in 1751: novices could only be received in houses of regular life on the Continent and needed the permission of the Nuncio at Brussels before they could return to Ireland on completion of their studies — further, a bishop had the power of veto over the movement of religious from his diocese. These Decrees represented over-reaction to undoubted abuses. They stifled religious life in Ireland, and the numerical strength of the friars began to decline. A fall in numbers of the diocesan clergy prompted a greater involvement of religious in running parishes. This eventually led to many situations of tension between the diocesan and regular clergy, especially towards the end of the century.

The Decrees of 1751 soon began to take effect. Appeals to Rome commenced and as a result we have a very good summary of the state of the Irish Franciscans in 1766. There were regular friaries at or near: Dublin, Kilkenny, Athlone, Multyfarnham, Wexford, Trim, Youghal, Cork, Waterford, Ennis, Limerick, Clonmel, Buttevant, Carrickbeg, Quin, Claregalway, Galway, Kilconnell, Elphin, Ross, Meelick, Kilnalahan, Drogheda, Armagh-Dungannon. However the communities were quite small, usually numbering only two or three friars, to a total of one hundred and nine, of whom about half were sick or elderly. There were about seventy five friars working in parishes, as well as about thirty five working outside of Ireland. This gives an approximate total of two hundred and twenty, compared with about five hundred and fifty during the first half of the century. By 1782, numbers had dropped to about one hundred and fifty. Rome relented somewhat in 1773, but the damage had already been done. Numbers continued to fall all during the next century, to reach an all-time low of about seventy five towards 1890 — but this is another story.

Living in hope . . .

The intermittent persecutions during the first half of the century, and the falling numbers of friars during the 1760's, meant that the eighteenth century was not a very happy one for the Irish

Franciscans. A few saw the solution of their personal problems in becoming involved with the Established Church: e.g. Mr Anthony Burke, who became a preacher at St Patrick's Cathedral, Dublin, in 1758. Most friars lived in hope, believing that things could hardly get worse.

With the advent of a new political enlightenment towards the end of the century, conditions did improve somewhat for Catholics in Ireland. Admittedly there were highly pragmatic reasons behind the new political moves. The Relief Act of 1782 enabled the friars to move with greater freedom and take on fresh apostolates. However, the confusion of the French Revolution was about to descend on Europe. For the Irish Franciscans, the result was a further period of turmoil during which their system of education on the Continent was practically destroyed and structure of their pastoral involvement in Ireland changed.

Graph of the Irish Franciscan Province from 1500 to date.

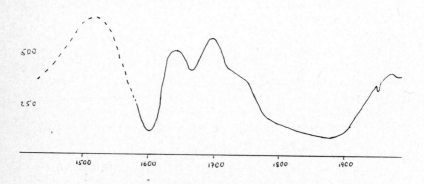

The number of Franciscans in the Irish Province.

The size of the Irish Franciscan Province peaked just before the Reformation, again during the seventeenth century, and finally in this century. Note the gradual decline from 1750 to 1900.

Chapter 7

THE PERIOD OF THE FRENCH REVOLUTION:
HOPE AND FRUSTRATION (1782-1830)

When the Relief Act was passed in 1782, the Franciscans hoped that they would now be free to lead a full religious and pastoral life. They hoped that they could also receive novices in Ireland. Yet these hopes were to be frustrated by the direct and indirect effects of the French Revolution. The Continental Colleges were closed. British political pressure resulted in the opening of Maynooth College and thus a re-organisation of the diocesan clergy in Ireland was undertaken, with the result that there was less scope for pastoral action by the friars. The continuing decline in vocations forced the abandonment of many old Franciscan areas in the country. The mild optimism of the 1820's, which gave rise to a major programme of re-building, was dampened by the attempted suppression of the regular orders, including the Franciscans, in the Catholic Emancipation Act of 1829. It took a number of years before the friars fully realised that the anti-religious section of this Act was largely inoperable.

The direct effects of the French Revolution

By 1780, the Irish Franciscans had come to depend very much on their Continental Colleges. While a small number of men were admitted to the novitiate in Ireland, most aspirants to the Order were sent to the Continent, usually to Louvain or Rome. They then completed their studies in these Colleges, or at Boulay, Capranica or Prague.

The first act which adversely affected the Continental Colleges was the religious policy of Joseph II of the Austro-Hungarian Empire. Prague was closed in 1786 due to his decisions, although some Irish friars remained active in the area until after the Napoleonic period. Louvain was kept open, despite attempts to close it. In the maelstorm of the French Revolution, Boulay was closed in 1792 and Louvain in the following year. Rome and Capranica were closed for longer or shorter periods, but were operating again by 1818. Some efforts were made to re-open Boulay. Even the trojan work of Fr Cowan ofm. failed to restore St Anthony's College in Louvain as an Irish Franciscan College. While the English Franciscans became virtually extinct due to the loss of their College at Douay, the Irish friars were able to survive due to their two houses in Italy.

The friars move out of parish work and diocesan involvement

A major sign of the new religious freedom of the period was the opening of St Patrick's College, Maynooth, in 1795. Even this event had political overtones typical of the age — one of the reasons for its foundation was to cut off the Irish clergy from the contaminating influence of continental revolutionary ideas. The first Professor of Scripture at Maynooth was an Irish Franciscan, Fr Thomas Clancy, who had been lecturing in Prague. Appointed in 1795, he resigned in 1797 to return to, and die in, his beloved Prague. The rise of Maynooth and the other Irish seminaries meant more diocesan clergy were available for parish duties. The friars moved to other activities.

In 1800 the friars were still at work in or near their old houses at Dublin, Wexford, Cashel (= Thurles), Claregalway, Athlone, Youghal, Limerick, Galway, Multyfarnham, Waterford, Clonmel, Meelick, Cork, Ennis, Carrickbeg, Drogheda and Ross; Dungannon, Trim, Jamestown, Buttevant, St John Baptist (= Edgeworthstown), Timoleague, Galbally (= Mitchelstown), Elphin, Killeigh, Monaghan, Cavan, Lisgoole, Donegal and about six other areas in Ulster. Of these thirty-six sites, the friars were still resident at only the first seventeen by 1830. There had been about seventy friars engaged in parish work in 1800, and this number had fallen to about five in 1830. One or two friars continued to be involved in parish work up to the 1860's.

The withdrawal of the friars from parish work was not without its problems. The most notorious of these was a dispute between the bishop of Cork and the four religious orders in the city about the obligation of religious to preach in the Cathedral. This dispute lasted for nearly thirty years until two decrees were issued from Rome in 1815. Further disputes involved the rights of the friars to have public churches rather than serving in parish churches.

The long line of Franciscan bishops in Ireland came to an end with Dr Patrick Maguire (coadjutor to Dr O'Reilly of Kilmore, 1818-26, but outlived by Dr O'Reilly). When Dr Touhy of Limerick requested in 1821, to the delight of many, that Fr William O'Meara ofm. be appointed his coadjutor, a strong clerical minority within the diocese objected so vehemently that Rome refused the request.

Franciscan life in Ireland about 1825

In these years, and for most of the nineteenth century, the friars lived and dressed more or less as diocesan priests, with house-keepers and servants to look after them. Brothers were practically unknown, although there were a number of perpetual tertiaries. The main pastoral role of the friars was to be available to people. If the friars had a church of their own, it was usually small. In the first quarter of the century, many friary churches were rebuilt (e.g. Carrickbeg & Athlone), sometimes on a new site (e.g. Limerick) or on the medieval site (e.g. Clonmel). Income came from stipends, questing (done after mass on Sundays), alms and a little manual work (especially market-gardening). Each friar looked after his own needs and there was no such thing as a community purse. Certain expenses, e.g. the wages of servants and the provincial tax for the support of St Isidore's in Rome, were paid jointly. Food and drink were matters for the individual. Typically these men had the Franciscan qualities of gentleness, kindness and courtesy to all, and were men of principle.

When the restrictions on the friars were eased in the early 1800's, one of the new apostolates which they took up was education. Schools were run by the First Order for varying periods during the century in such places as Athlone, Carrickbeg, Clonmel, Dalkey, Killarney, Limerick, Multyfarnham and Wexford. Since there was such a small number of friars in each community, they had to employ lay teachers to help staff these schools. The present 'Monks of the West' (Third Order Brothers of Mountbellew) originated in this fashion.

Formation usually began with a year's novitiate in Ireland (Cork in the 1810's, then Wexford). Solemn vows were taken immediately after the novitiate, since the period of simple profession was only introduced in 1859. After the novitiate, the cleric went to Rome for three or four years of study. Having entered the Order about the age of sixteen, he was usually ordained about the age of twenty.

Political involvement

Given the temper of the period, it was natural for the more energetic friars to become involved in politics. Fr Denis Taaffe is reputed to have commanded a company of the Insurgents in 1798. More important was the involvement of Fr Richard Hayes with the anti-Veto agitation in 1815. The English politicians were willing to grant concessions provided they were allowed a veto in the appointment of bishops. Fr Hayes, a Wexfordman, spent two years in Rome petitioning the Holy See not to concede the power of veto to the government. His mission ended in confusion and Daniel O'Connell eventually paid part of the bill for his expenses.

O'Connell had a friendly relationship with the Franciscans. The head of Fr Francis O'Sullivan ofm., who had been killed while saying mass in 1653, probably on Scariff Island in Kenmare Bay, was a family possession. The head was stolen in 1847, but mysteriously returned to Killarney friary in 1931. In the 1820's O'Connell gave much helpful advice to the friars, especially when they were engaged in re-building some of their churches. His life-long friend, Fr Roger O'Higgins ofm., was largely responsible for the monument to O'Connell erected in Limerick in 1857.

The problem of Catholic Emancipation

Catholic Emancipation was politically motivated, and the bill approving it was only passed by a suspicious parliament and an eccentric king after certain precautions had been taken. The loss of the franchise by small freeholders is quite well known, but not many people realise that the entire second half of the Emancipation Bill contained legislation by which regulars and Jesuits would be forced into extinction. All friars in the country were to register, all novitiates were to close, no further friars would be allowed to return from the Continent and thus the religious orders would slowly die out. Only female orders and diocesan congregations would survive.

This legislation was the equivalent of that which led to the suppression of the Jesuits on the Continent. The passing of the Emancipation Bill in 1829 caused dismay among the friars. They had second thoughts about plans for expansion and re-building. Despite the assurances of Daniel O'Connell that the law could not and would not be enforced, it took a number of years before the friars felt safe again. In fact the law was enforced, but only in a very limited number of cases dealing with charitable bequests and with the payment of rates. Although removed from the English Statute Book, this legislation is law in Ireland and has a few practical applications. By it the friars are still, in theory, outlaws.

Mission to Newfoundland

A typical result of the hope which the Irish Franciscans felt about 1780 was the opening of their first foreign mission — to Newfoundland. About 1763 almost a third of the population there were Irish-speaking catholics, suffering from neglect and semi-official persecution. Even though some French Franciscans were working there, the Irish quite often, incredibly, travelled all the way back to Ireland to receive the sacraments. In January 1784, three Waterford-men applied to London for a permanent priest to look after them in Newfoundland. The British Government approved of their request. Before the year was out an Irish Franciscan, Fr James Louis O'Donnell, arrived as Prefect Apostolic. A native of Knocklofty, Co. Tipperary, he had studied in Rome and Prague before his ordination in 1770. He was Minister Provincial in 1779-82. After his arrival in

Newfoundland, other friars came to help him. The Prefecture became a Vicariate on 5th. Jan. 1796 and Fr O'Donnell was consecrated bishop at Quebec on 21st. Sept. 1796. He resigned in 1807 and returned to Ireland, where he died in 1811.

The next bishop was Dr Patrick Lambert, who had been Irish Franciscan Provincial in 1803-04. He had been coadjutor since 1806 and he resigned in 1817. His place was taken by another Irish friar, Dr Thomas Scallan, who had gone to Newfoundland in 1812. On his death in 1830, he was succeeded by Dr Michael Anthony Fleming, who had come to Newfoundland as a missionary in 1823. An energetic friar, Dr Fleming began to seek new missionaries in Ireland, among both his own Franciscans and the diocesan clergy. Before his death in 1850 he had begun to build the cathedral. The last of the Irish Franciscan bishops in Newfoundland, Dr Thomas Mullock, had been coadjutor since 1847. His major contribution before his death in 1869 was the foundation of a local seminary. Circumstances in Ireland had never permitted more than a handful of Irish friars to go as missionaries — between two and five at any given time. The local seminary led to a growth in the local clergy. Irish Franciscan connections with Newfoundland ceased, for all practical purposes, in 1877, when Fr P. A. Slattery, having previously resigned as President of the local seminary, returned to Europe. Another Irish friar volunteered to go to Newfoundland, but was not sent. Fr Slattery was proposed as Bishop of Harbour Grace in 1880, but not appointed. A hundred years of Irish Franciscan work in Newfoundland had ended.

Activities in far-flung fields

While the mission in Newfoundland was the main centre for Irish Franciscan work outside of Ireland, individual friars tried to bring Christ to people in many parts of the world. Fr Michael Egan ofm., who had been working in Philadelphia since 1803, became its first bishop in 1808. Fr Patrick Murphy ofm. spent most of his life in Jamaica and Trinidad, while Fr Hatton Walsh worked initially at Grenada, later in Halifax and possibly even on the Falkland Islands. Fr Daniel Burke died in S. Africa in 1839. Fr Charles Maguire, who had worked mainly around Pittsburgh, was proposed for an American bishopric in 1817. Fr T. Quigley died in Ireland in 1804 having worked initially in London and later in the West Indies. Even two Provincials of the Irish friars seem to have occupied that office while living abroad: Fr Anthony Coen as a parish priest in London (1801-03) and Fr James Cowan while trying to re-open St Anthony's College at Louvain (1819-22).

47

Since the time of St Francis, the Franciscans have been especially concerned with looking after the Holy Places. The Custody of the Holy Land is a completely international unit within the Franciscan Order, and many Irish friars have laboured there. Thus, during this time, Fr Aloysius Stafford served in Jerusalem for eight years, Fr Joseph (Louis) Lynch taught English at a school in Aleppo, while Fr Augustine Holohan served in Cyprus.

From 1782 to 1830 the Irish Franciscans seem to have been ready and willing to undertake any task, any place, any time. Their misfortune seems to have been that circumstances, especially lack of numbers, were against them. The hopes of 1782 had faded, but by 1830 the possibilities for the future were promising.

Waterford Friary: Snipe

Chapter 8

A PERIOD OF SEARCHING FOR A WAY OF LIFE (1830-1899)

By the time the fears of friars about the anti-religious legislation of 1829 had faded, the position of the Franciscans in Ireland had been consolidated. The decline in vocations had more or less ceased. The smaller houses had been closed down. St Isidore's College in Rome was functioning normally. The friars were well liked by the people. There were no real financial worries. However, the level of community life and of regular observance was extremely low and it would be hard to distinguish the way of life of a Franciscan from that of a diocesan priest.

Religious life on the Continent had undergone sweeping changes due to the French Revolution. Whole Franciscan provinces had been wiped out. The key to renewal and rebuilding had been found in 'regular observance' — an insistence on the importance of external behaviour as a sign of religious witness. The man of external discipline was bound to be a true christian within. The logical conclusion of this movement on the Continent was the extreme Ultramontanism of the late nineteenth and early twentieth centuries.

The concept of regular observance was strange to the Irish Franciscans. Since they enjoyed the confidence of people, they saw no reason for changing their way of life. Their history from 1830 to the end of the century is the story of how Continental pressures forced them to see the value of regular observance and put it into practice in their lives.

First attempts at reform: Fr Henry Hughes ofm.

Fr Henry Hughes became Provincial of the Irish Franciscans in 1837. There were sixteen houses in Ireland with about fifty-five priests. Practically all the buildings had been renovated within the previous ten years and the last closure of a house (Ross) had taken place in 1832. The students were trained in Rome. Capranica had been rented out in order to provide finances for the students. The mission in Newfoundland was prospering under Dr Fleming, while the first Irish Franciscans would soon depart for Australia.

The Minister General, Fr Bartholomew Altemir, wrote to Fr Hughes on 3rd. September 1837, drawing his attention to certain matters. As Fr Hughes passed through the friaries on visitation, he imposed various obligations mentioned in the General's letter: proper care of the churches, attention to saying mass correctly, community meditation, common recitation of the Divine Office, proper libraries and archives, and a need for theological conferences.

Fr Hughes went to Rome in 1839 about problems between the friars of Waterford and the local bishop. While there, he was appointed Vicar Apostolic of Gibraltar, where he became the first non-Spanish bishop. Gibraltar had just been split off from the diocese of Cadiz and Dr Hughes became a sort of British public hero due to his harassment by the Spanish and by some local Catholics. He resigned about 1845 and retired to Ireland, where he died in 1860.

Irish Franciscans in Australia

The first Irish Franciscan missionary departed for Australia while Fr Hughes was Provincial. However, the first Irish friar associated with the provision of priests for Australia was Fr Richard Hayes. Following the receipt of information from his elder brother, who had been living in the country for seventeen years, Fr Hayes petitioned Rome for priests for Australia in 1816. The priest who was sent out was the legendary Fr Jeremiah Flynn o.cist. Slowly an official attitude of opposition to a catholic clergy lessened and a number of priests, many of them English Benedictines, were recruited.

During a trip to Europe, Fr Ullathorne, then V.G. of Sydney, recruited a number of Irish priests. Many of these were secular, but two of them were Irish Franciscans. Fr Patrick (Bonaventure) Geoghegan ofm. left Ireland in November 1838 and travelled to Australia with Fr Ullathorne. Initially he worked in the Melbourne region but he later became the second bishop of Adelaide (1859-64). The second Irish friar, Fr Nicholas Coffey, went to Australia in 1842 and worked mainly in Sydney and at Parramatta up to the time of his death in 1857. The pattern of individual friars going to help in particular areas continued. Thus Fr Patrick (Bonaventure) Shiel, who arrived to work in Melbourne in 1853, was appointed bishop of Adelaide in 1864, in succession to Dr Geoghegan. Dr Shiel died in 1872.

As yet there was no Franciscan community in Australia. As early as 1871 Dr Shiel had ambitions in this direction, but only on the understanding that the friars could live a proper community life. One energetic friar — Fr Peter (Francis) O'Farrell — had been working earnestly for such a Franciscan foundation. Born outside Athlone in 1809, he entered the Order at St Isidore's, Rome, in 1832. As we shall see later, he was Commissary Visitator of the Irish Province in 1852 and tried to reform the friars in Ireland. He went to Australia in 1854. From then until his death while on holiday in Ireland in 1874 he encouraged every move for a permanent Franciscan community in

Australia. In particular he saved up all his spare funds for this purpose.

Soon after Fr O'Farrell's death, Dr Roger Bede Vaughan, coadjutor to the Archbishop of Sydney, opened negotiations for a foundation in the archdiocese. The Irish Provincial Definitory agreed in principle in 1876, but it was March 1879 before the first two friars, Frs Peter (James) Hanrahan and Martin (Augustine) Holohan, set sail. The final agreement was not signed until 6th. June 1879. The community, based in Waverly, rapidly built up to six friars. From Waverly they staffed two residences, at Paddington and Woolahara.

The total number of friars in Australia increased very slowly. By 1908 there were still only nine friars (including two on loan from the English Province), but the first Australian students were near ordination. Despite frantic appeals in various quarters, it was only well after the First World War that friars began to arrive in satisfactory numbers. The scattered houses in Australia and New Zealand were erected into the Franciscan Province of the Holy Spirit on 31st. Oct. 1939. New Zealand had started as an Italian Franciscan mission and the first Irish friar to help there had been Fr James (Anthony) Mahony in 1867. In 1939 there were only one hundred and twenty three religious in the new province, which had eight houses. Because of the Second World War, arrangements for the full transfer of authority from the Irish friars were not completed until 1949.

Second attempt at reform: Dr Cullen and Fr O'Farrell in 1852

After Fr Hughes had departed for Gibralter, the friars reverted to their old ways. No real changes were made. Most interest seems to have been focused on elections at the provincial chapters. In 1850 there was a big discussion about the custom of eating meat on Saturdays. In the meantime, the National Synod had been held at Thurles and a number of conscientious friars were a little worried about their way of life. One of these, Fr Peter (Francis) O'Farrell, was appointed visitor of the Irish Province in 1852.

Fr O'Farrell's first effort was to try to enforce the decrees made by Fr Hughes. In this he used further letters from the Minister General and the decisions of the Synod of Thurles. He also added some ideas of his own, in particular the wearing of the habit both inside and outside the friary. The Provincial Chapter following the visitation broke up in disarray as Fr O'Farrell, supported by the new Archbishop of Dublin, Dr Cullen, tried to force his ideas on the friars. The Minister General had to appoint the new superiors of the

Province. Fr O'Farrell went to Australia, where he continued to work for 'regular observance'. The friars returned to their former way of life. Dr Cullen began to think of the reform 'of a certain religious order', i.e. the Franciscans.

From 1852 until his death in 1878, Dr Cullen was active in the domain of religious life, using his title of Apostolic Visitator of the Religious of Ireland. In practice, he kept an eye on the friars who were likely to become provincials. He insisted that the visitator general confer with him during the visitation. Dr Cullen would then decided whether the visitator could hold the provincial chapter, in which case the superiors would be elected, or should hold a provincial congregation, in which case the superiors would be appointed from Rome, often on the recommendation of Dr Cullen himself. The Franciscan authorities in Rome, who also wished to reform the Irish Province, but in their own way, quietly counter-acted Dr Cullen's efforts. By 1870 they were able to by-pass him.

Belgian efforts at reform: Fr van Loo in 1857

In the aftermath of the French Revolution, the Belgian Franciscan Province had become extinct and was re-established in 1842. The loss of the English Franciscan College at Douay had been followed by the repression of religious in England under Catholic Emancipation. As a result, the English Province had no novitiate, and was reduced to four members by 1850. Contact was established between the remaining English friars and the young vigorous Belgian Province through the Franciscan nuns at Taunton in 1848. A decade passed before the Belgians had sufficient priests to make their first foundation in England at Sclerder. After years of steady progress, a full English Province was re-erected in 1891.

The Belgian friar most associated with England was Fr Bernard van Loo. A native of Ghent, he had been a diocesan priest before joining the Belgian friars in 1844. He came to England in 1849 to negotiate the coming of the Belgian Franciscans and he was insistent that the key to Franciscan life was a pure observance of the Rule. At the General Chapter at Rome in 1856 — the first full chapter for nearly a hundred years — he made quite an impression, and was elected Procurator General of the Recollects and Alcantarines. He was appointed Visitator General and Reformer of the Irish Province in 1857.

Fr van Loo conducted a quick, vigorous and efficient visitation in each friary. He spelt out the current abuses in short, crisp terms. He persuaded the Provincial Chapter and Definitory to accept a special set of statutes for Ireland, based on a summary of General legislation and on the statutes for Belgium. He broke the tradition of electing the provincial successively from each civil province and of having a provincial definitor from each province as well. In fact the new Provincial was not elected, but was very carefully chosen by Rome. He was Fr L. Cosgrove, and was picked for his personal dedication to reform. Within a few years the new Provincial had arranged for the opening of a strict novitiate at Drogheda. He promulgated new regulations for the students in Rome. He further rationalised the number of friaries in Ireland with the aim of concentrating the remaining friars in larger communities where they could lead a common life. Thus there was no effort to re-open Meelick (closed 1853), the community in Claregalway was withdrawn to Galway (1858 — but they continued to say mass on Sundays in the old church for a number of years), Youghal friary at Aglish was closed in 1862 and it took the personal intervention of the archbishop of Cashel to keep Thurles open (1860).

Fr van Loo had used his visit to Ireland to make arrangements for the first new house of the Belgians in England. Before he left Ireland, he also decided that the Belgian Franciscans would open a house at Gorey. He had arranged the reform of the Irish Province by introducing new legislation and by carefully picking the superiors. He also wished that the Irish would be reformed by the good example of the new Belgian community at Gorey. The first friars arrived there in October 1858. They acted as chaplains to the Ram family and to the Franciscan Sisters of Perpetual Adoration. It proved impossible to turn Gorey into an ideal Franciscan house. On the invitation of the bishop, Dr Moriarty, the friars moved to Killarney in July 1860. The new friary there became the novitiate of the English Province. One of the Irishmen who joined the English friars through Killarney was Fr David Fleming. He became a noted theologian, deeply involved in the theological controversies of his times. He was a member of the various commissions on Anglican Orders, of the Biblical Commission and of other Papal bodies in Rome. He was the first Provincial of the newly erected English Province in 1891 and governed the whole Order as Vicar General in 1901-3. He played a significant part in the handing over of Killarney to the Irish friars in 1902.

After Fr van Loo left Ireland, he kept in contact with the situation and used his influence in Rome to keep up pressure for reform. A succession of visitators kept harping on the same points time and time again: divine office in choir, annual retreats, monthly recollection, theological conferences, Stations of the Cross, the giving of missions and retreats, etc. Propaganda Fide, then the competent Roman authority for the Irish Church, was brought into the picture more and more. Thus the use of titular guardianates, as a result of which practically every priest in the Province was entitled to attend the

Provincial Chapter, ceased in 1873 by order of the Minister General, backed by Propaganda.

The will to reform began to grow within the Province, although this was not to show itself fully until the Provincialate of Fr Alphonsus Jackman (1882-88 & 1895-99). The friars were caught up in the spirit of Vatican 1, just as the friars today have been inspired by Vatican 2. The stress was on 'precise doctrines on papal authority . . . ., a more authoritive and centralised church structure . . . , a new piety, which insisted more on reception of the sacraments and multiplicity of external practices than on interior piety' (Roger Aubert). However, the friars were slow to move. The visitators continued to press for reform and found a new abuse which they wished to stamp out — the presence of female cooks and housekeepers in the friaries.

Under German influence: Fr Gregor Janknecht (1879) . . .

Like the Belgian Province, the German provinces had been hard hit by the French Revolution. The Province of Saxony had never died out, although it had come very close to doing so. From 1850 on, it was in the process of re-building and expanding under Fr Gregor Janknecht (Provincial 1855-61, 1867-79 and 1888-91, Definitor General 1862-67). Fr Janknecht sent the first group of German friars to the U.S.A., where they eventually founded the Sacred Heart Province. He was appointed Visitator General of the Irish Province in 1879 and again in 1888. Both visits were highly significant. During his first visitation he was willing to tolerate the level of reform that had been achieved in Ireland until a number of small incidents persuaded him that radical reform was essential. During his second visitation he gave further impetus to the reform which he had begun.

. . . and Fr Joseph (Bernard) Doebbing (1883)

About this time, the Kulturkampf had interrupted Franciscan life in Germany and a number of students, including one Joseph (Bernard) Doebbing, fled to the U.S.A. to finish their studies. Son of a Münster cobbler, Fr Doebbing had joined the friars in 1873 at the age of eighteen. Following his ordination, he did higher studies and was transferred to the Franciscan House of Studies at Quaracchi, near Florence, in 1881. There he met, probably by arrangement with Fr Janknecht, Fr Luke Carey, Guardian of St Isidore's College. Fr Luke was a keen reformer in his own right and was looking for lectors to train students at St Isidore's. He was impressed by Fr Doebbing and invited him to come to Rome and help in reforming the young Irish friars. The Minister General was delighted, since such a move fitted in well with the reform of the whole Irish Province.

Fr Doebbing was appointed lector at St Isidore's on 10th. October 1883. He became master of students on 5th. December. He tried the experiment of sending the students to the College of Propaganda Fide, but they found the course there too difficult. A group of German brothers arrived to look after the needs of the community at St Isidore's. They were soon followed by a group of German students and lectors, so that the Irish clerics could be taught regular life by example and given lectures in theology within the college. Some financial aid was also sent from Germany to help in the up-keep. The more turbulent Irish students were sent to spend some time in smaller Italian friaries.

At the suggestion of the Minister General, who was encouraged by Fr Janknecht, the Irish Provincial Chapter of 1885 agreed to send the Irish postulants to do their novitiate under German control, mainly at the new novitiate of the Saxony Province at Harreveld in Holland. In 1888 Fr Janknecht came as Visitator to Ireland for the second time. Then, with the consent of Propaganda Fide, the Minister General unveiled his plan for the total reform of the Irish Province: no novices could be received in Ireland for six years; Fr Doebbing was appointed Delegate General for St Isidore's, where the rights of the Irish Province would be suspended for the time being (this appointment was later extended to cover Capranica and the new foundation at S. Elia); newly ordained priests would be kept on the Continent until there was a sufficient number to take over two houses in Ireland, one of which would then become the novitiate; the older friars would be allowed to die out peacefully, as the new friars took over the Province house by house. The old friars had no choice but to agree.

The Irish Provincial, Fr Jackman, did go to Rome to appeal to Propaganda, apparently in ignorance of the procedures which had been followed. He pointed to the considerable progress towards a complete reform which had been made by the older friars. At the General Congregation of Propaganda Fide on 1st. April 1889, the Cardinals unanimously backed the action of the Minister General. There could be no further appeal.

Individual reactions to the imposition of reform

The Minister General was delighted. He recalled the success of the Belgian-English house in Killarney and he praised the old friars for their efforts to reform. In particular he was grateful that all housekeepers and female cooks had gone from the friaries. He was sure that the friars would be pleased with the complete reform which was now to be imposed.

Fr Janknecht was content that the re-vitalised Province of Saxony had been healthy enough to cure an ailing sister Province. Fr Doebbing was satisfied with the course things had taken. He resigned from St Isidore's in 1898, became involved in affairs at the Franciscan Curia and was nominated bishop of Nepi and Sutri on 1st. April 1900. Being a German bishop in an Italian diocese, he came under very heavy criticism during the First World War. He died on 14th. March 1916, having been a capable administrator of his diocese for sixteen years.

Fr Luke Carey was happy that his efforts to improve standards of theology at St Isidore's had succeeded. However, he was a little annoyed at what he considered the drastic treatment of the Irish Province and he left St Isidore's. Unfortunately a bitter row broke out when he was falsely accused of mal-administration and this soured his later years.

Fr Jackman, the Provincial, and most of the older friars felt peeved at the way the reform had been pushed through. They had done their best, but they could not see that this was not enough. Their circumstances had made them blind to the true meaning of reform: e.g. they had understood 'a reform of the novitiate' to mean building a new novitiate in Ennis, and not to mean training the novices in a new spirit. Most of them were happy enough to be let die in peace. A number joined the new reformers when they arrived in Ireland. Some did leave the Province, or the Order, to work as priests elsewhere. From 1890 on, the old friars concentrated their efforts on making sure that the Germans would not.retain St Isidore's and Capranica. They did not mind the Germans retaining the new foundation at S. Elia.

The Reform comes to Ireland

The last non-reform Irish Provincial Chapter met in 1895. The first group of reformers, Frs Peter Begley and Nicholas Dillon, with two other priests and two brothers, returned to Ireland in 1896. Despite a short last stand by the old friars, the new friars were able to take over Multyfarnham as the first House of the reform on 11th. December 1896.

1897 was an important year for the Franciscan Order, since in that year Leo XIII promulgated a uniform set of General Constitutions for the whole Order, doing away with the distinctions between Observant and Reformed, Discalced and Recollect.

A provincial chapter was due in 1899, but permission to hold it was refused. On 2nd. March 1899, the General Definitorium, by virtue of a rescript of Propaganda Fide, appointed a new Provincial administration: Fr Peter Begley as Provincial, Fr Bernard Cooney (a firm favourite of the 'old' friars) as Custos, and four Definitors. The Minister General laid down the basic rules in his letter promulgating the appointments: the General Constitutions were to be observed; certain houses were to be given to the new friars (the junior fathers, or brown friars, since they wore brown habits); those who wished to continue in the old way of life (the senior fathers, or black friars, since they dressed in black clerical suits) were to be assigned to special convents; provisional decisions were to be made about a seraphic college to educate young aspirants (Multyfarnham), a novitiate (initially Ennis, later Killarney) and a student house (Rome). At this time only Multyfarnham and Ennis had been taken over, soon to be followed by Athlone, while Cork had been designated as the friary where the old friars who wished to live a strict life could stay. The date of this decree, 2nd. March 1899, may be taken as the day when the Irish Province stopped searching for a new way of life and discovered a new expression of Franciscanism.

Askeaton Friary

Chapter 9

THE FRIARS APPLY THE PRINCIPLES OF VATICAN I (1899-1972)

As the Brown Franciscans took over the friaries in Ireland one by one, they discovered the tremendous amount of good-will which the people had towards the Black friars. Many of these old friars are still remembered by the people of friary towns: e.g. people in Thurles still talk about Fr Mick or Fr Mack (Fr James Theodosius McNamara, died 1881), while those in Carrick-on-Suir remember Fr Thomas (Joseph) Rossiter, who died in 1928. At the turn of the century there were about one hundred and ten friars in the Province and about seven novices joined each year. There were about ten friars engaged on the Australian mission, where the first local vocations were beginning to emerge. There were thirteen friaries in Ireland (Thurles had been closed in 1892, and Killarney handed over to the Irish in 1902), two on the Continent and three in Australia. Most of the friars were Munstermen, mainly from Clare and Limerick.

Franciscan life in Ireland in the early twentieth century

The new Brown friars were typical of the Catholic Church in the era following the First Vatican Council. The stress was on centralised government. This produced long series of rules and regulations which enabled the individual friar to discover what was the will of God for him in any aspect of life. Formal devotions were introduced and much appreciated by the people. The Brown friars were responding to the mood of the Irish Church. As more young priests and brothers came back from the Continent, the friaries in Ireland were taken over one by one, Cork finally in 1910, Wexford and Galway in 1918, Drogheda slightly later, while Waterford was the last house to change, in 1927.

The reform did run into some problems. A number of the Black friars opted to become diocesan priests or military chaplains. The attitude of the friar who was elected Minister Provincial in 1911, Fr John Capistran Hanrahan, was considered not quite correct and he was replaced by Fr Nicholas Dillon in 1912. Strange to relate, Fr John was appointed the next Provincial in 1918 and then supervised some of the final regulations about the wearing of the habit, etc. The opening of St Anthony's Hall in Cork in 1909 enabled the young Franciscan students to attend U.C.C., but it was too early yet for such a move and the Hall was closed after a couple of years. While the reform movement may seem dour and cold at a first glance, the rough exterior of many of the Brown friars was soon broken by their Irish humanity and they emerged as 'characters' in their own right.

Increase in size of the Province: fresh apostolates

As with most other orders, vocations to the Irish Franciscans rose rapidly after the First World War. In round figures, the number of friars increased from one hundred and ten in 1900, to one hundred and fifty by 1920, to two hundred and twenty five in 1930 and to two hundred and fifty by 1945. By 1960 the total had reached the four hundred mark, to eventually peak at four hundred and thirty in 1965. This represented a return to the high figures of the early 1700's. Numbers have declined slightly since and now seem to be levelling off at about three hundred and seventy five.

Due to the lack of manpower, the Irish friars were not greatly involved in the turbulent events of 1914-18. A very few friars did serve as chaplains to armies in various parts of the world. Similarly the events of 1916-21 in Ireland had very little direct influence on the friars. A hall at Merchant's Quay, Dublin, was used for IRA training before 1916. Individual friars were involved in the Republican movement on a personal basis. Perhaps the most famous of these was the young Fr Philip Murphy. His intense interest in social problems and his work in labour relations led to his appointment as chaplain to the mayors of Limerick. In this capacity he was deeply involved in the 'Murdered Mayors' incident in 1921, following which British pressure forced him to leave the city. After tremendous work in other parts of Ireland, he went to Australia in 1933, where he died in 1954.

The increase in vocations after 1920 enabled the friars to extend their apostolates. Initially student houses had to be re-organised. Thus the old College of St Anthony at Louvain in Belgium was bought back by the friars after a gap of a century and re-opened in 1926 as a house of philosophy and theology. St Anthony's College, Galway, opened in 1932. As a result, many friars were able to take degree courses at U.C.G. St Anthony's College became really important during the Second World War, when Louvain had to be evacuated and communication with Rome became extremely difficult. The re-opening of the college in Louvain was symptomatic of another interest of the friars of the 1920's — an awareness of the history of the Irish Franciscans, and especially their important contribution to life, religion and politics in seventeenth century Ireland. Thus the new friary church at Athlone was built to honour the Four Masters. Later on the new friary at Rossnowlagh was seen as the re-incarnation of

Donegal friary, while a special institute for research into Irish Franciscan History and Irish culture was founded at Killiney in 1945.

Increased manpower meant greater pastoral opportunities. The more normal routine of mass and confession was supplemented by popular devotions, novenas, etc. The Franciscan tradition of giving parish missions and retreats was re-enforced. Pilgrimages were organised, not only to the more popular places such as Lourdes and Rome, but also to several of the old Franciscan sites in Ireland. Friars became involved in the mass media, especially in the field of the printed word. Many of the old friary churches were re-built or enlarged (Athlone, Carrick-on-Suir, Cork, Drogheda, Dublin, Limerick and Waterford), while a new friary was founded at Rossnowlagh in 1946. Education became an important apostolate. A Seraphic College, or minor seminary, was started at Multyfarnham in October 1899, and became a normal boarding school when it was moved to Gormanston in 1956. Multyfarnham then became an agricultural college. A number of friars were appointed to posts at university level, especially at U.C.G. More recently, many friars have been giving religious instruction at technical, vocational and secondary schools.

Professed brothers were introduced into the Irish Province by the Brown friars. There had been brothers previously — the famous Michael O'Cleary was a brother — but the tradition had died out by the nineteenth century. The place of the brother was taken by the perpetual tertiary. During the Reform under Fr Doebbing, a number of Irish lay-novices were given special training both in the spiritual life and in trades by German brothers. These Irishmen served as a basis on which the life-style of the brothers in the Irish Province has been built for the last fifty years.

Foreign missions in the twentieth century

When the number of friars in Ireland had risen sufficiently, greater attention could be given to missionary work abroad. There had been a small number of Irish Franciscans in Australia. From about 1925 on, local vocations increased and more Irishmen were sent out, so that Australia and New Zealand became the independent Province of the Holy Spirit in 1939.

The Minister General in Rome brought pressure on the Irish friars to open a mission in the Far East. He favoured a mission in the Philippines, but the Irish Provincial, acting on the advice of Fr Maurice Connaughton, an Irish friar who had been working in China for years, decided that it would be better to help the Venetian Franciscans in Hupeh, where they had charge of the Vicariate of

Hankow under Dr Eugenio Massi ofm. The first group of seven Irish friars arrived at Shanghai on 18th. December 1935. The Irish Franciscan Chinese mission became independent when part of the Vicariate was split off as the Prefecture Apostolic of Suihsien, with Fr Maurice as Prefect, on 17th. June 1937. Within a number of years the Prefecture had some twenty four chapels, eighty out-stations, schools and a minor seminary at Anlu.

Almost from the start, the mission was in a war zone with Japanese, Chinese regular and Chinese communist armies passing through the region. From 1938 to 1946 some fifteen Irish friars, four Chinese secular priests and three Chinese Franciscan priests carried on as best they could. The end of the Second World War saw the beginning of the Chinese Civil War and the 'Reds' occupied Anlu by August 1947. Although further missionaries were on their way from Ireland, the situation became impossible and a decision was taken to close the mission in November 1948. However the last of the missionaries did not cross over into Hong Kong until Easter 1951. A number of Chinese friars remained and one, Fr Dominic Ch'en, took over as Apostolic Administrator on 5th. April 1951. The Procuration at Hong Kong, from which many of the Franciscan missions in China were supplied, was run by the Irish Province from 1936 to 1939 and again from 1950, when it was re-opened to help expelled missionaries.

The closure of the mission in China dove-tailed neatly with the beginning of a new missionary effort in Africa. The Bavarian Franciscans had taken over the Vicariate of Kokstad, named after a local coloured hero, Adam Kok, from the Marianhill Fathers, following its erection as a vicariate on 11th. July 1939. The bishop, eight priest and four brothers, all German, were interned during World War II. Afterwards the mother province was too depleted in numbers to fulfill its commitments. The Irish friars accepted a call for help and the first four missionaries, accompanied by the Minister Provincial, arrived at Kokstad on 27th. December 1946. Three more arrived in 1947. In this same year there was an unsuccessful attempt to help at St Albert's College, Ernakulam, Cochin, in India. The Irish friars were requested, by the Apostolic Delegate in S. Africa, to staff a new seminary. A temporary building was acquired at Queenstown, near Port Elizabeth, and opened on 14th. April 1948. The foundation stone of a permanent building was laid on 26th. February 1950 in Pretoria, and the new seminary opened there on 1st. March 1951.

The mission in Kokstad progressed slowly but surely. The Irish Provincial, Fr Evangelist McBride, was consecrated bishop of the Vicariate on 25th. July 1949. Kokstad became a diocese following

61

the erection of a national hierarchy in S. Africa on 11th. January 1951. It is still cared for by Irish Franciscans. Also in S. Africa, the friars accepted the invitation of the bishop of Durban to make a foundation in his diocese in 1958. In another part of S. Africa the Irish Franciscans agreed to a request from the bishop of Johannesburg to take over some townships around the city. As a result the friars now have six houses in the Transvaal, where they are engaged in a wide variety of apostolates. Another episcopal invitation brought the Irish Franciscans into Rhodesia, where they took over a section of the diocese of Salisbury from the Jesuits, who wished to concentrate their efforts in other areas. The first contract was signed on 4th. July 1958 and the friars now have a foundation in Salisbury and a huge mission area to the south of the city. Recently arrangements have been made in conjunction with the English Franciscans, who also have missions in S. Africa, for the eventual establishment of a unified Franciscan presence in that country. A novitiate and a student house are already functioning.

In common with other religious orders, the Irish friars turned their attention towards Latin America in the 1960's. From 1964 one Irish friar lived in Chile helping Franciscans in that country. Following protracted negotiations, more friars went out to help in April 1968, again with the aim of assisting the Chilean Province. This arrangement has now (1977) been terminated. During the Second Vatican Council, negotiations began with the bishop of San Salvador for a mission in part of his diocese. The first group left Ireland for this mission in 1968 and it has proved a difficult assignment. A small band of Irish friars now have responsibility for a huge area centred on the town of Gotera. There are a number of Irish Franciscans working on their own in South America.

In addition to all this missionary activity organised by the Irish Province, individual Irish Franciscans continue to serve in many odd corners of the world where there is a need for them. Thus a number of Irishmen have served in the Franciscan Custody of the Holy Land. Others have worked in places with such romantic names as Taipeohsien (Formosa) and Mogadiscio (Somalia).

Reaction to Vatican 2

The Catholic world of 1960 was a comfortable place, especially in an Ireland preparing to celebrate the Patrician Year. The Irish Franciscans were working effectively, leading a good regular life and extending a helping hand to all in need. They were imbued with the spirit of Vatican I. Fr Celsus O'Brien was elected Minister Provincial at the Chapter in 1960 and remained in charge until 1972. His twelve years in office conveniently straddle the period of change associated with Vatican 2. By 1972 the surface changes associated with the Ecumenical Council had taken place and a deeper appreciation of what these implied was beginning to emerge.

The initial Irish Franciscan reaction to Pope John's Council was excitement, coupled with a traditional desire to follow the latest instructions from Rome. Two members of the Irish Province were periti. The first changes were taken up with enthusiasm, especially as regards the liturgy — changing around sanctuaries for mass facing the people, saying mass in English and Irish, etc. Some friars got deeply involved in youth work, in discussion groups and in lectures on the spirit of the Council.

It took some time before the deeper implications of the Council began to dawn on the friars. Some were understandably fearful, but most became aware of the Holy Spirit working in the Church. Thus it became evident that liturgical changes were not just about altars facing the people, but were about a different approach to prayer. The period of maximum confusion was in the late 1960's and early 1970's. The changes in the Church still clashed with the deeper feelings of many sincere christians and friars. A sign of this uncertainty was the sharp decline in vocations. By 1972 a keener appreciation of what was happening had begun to emerge. The confusion decreased and vocations began to return to normal. The Irish Franciscans had begun to transform themselves into friars imbued with the spirit of Vatican 2.

Dromahair Friary: Skillet

63

Chapter 10

OTHER IRISH MEMBERS OF THE
FRANCISCAN FAMILY

While this book has been concerned mainly with the history of the
Order of Friars Minor in Ireland, it would be unfair not to mention
the religious in other orders and congregations which also trace their
origins back to Saint Francis of Assisi. The Franciscan family is
divided into three orders: the First Order for men, the Second Order
for women, and the Third Order, which was initially for the laity. The
First Order is composed of three independent orders, each with equal
rights and privileges: the Friars Minor (i.e. those whose history in
Ireland we have been following); the Friars Minor Conventual (who
shared in the history of the Franciscans in medieval times, but who
died out in Ireland during the Reformation); the Friars Minor
Capuchins. The Second Order in Ireland, the Poor Clares, called
after St Clare of Assisi, is composed of two independent groups, both
of whom have a common origin. The Third Order Regular, i.e. those
religious who base their lives on the rule written by St Francis for the
laity, is made up of quite a large number of congregations.

1. The Friars Minor Capuchins

The Irish Province of the Capuchins has seven houses in Ireland
(two in Dublin, three in Cork, one each in Kilkenny and Donegal)
with a vice-province on the Pacific Coast of the U.S.A., a district in
New Zealand and missions in Zambia and S. Africa. The total
number of friars is just under three hundred, of whom about half live
in Ireland.

Irish Capuchin history begins with Fr Francis Nugent (better
known as Friar Nugent), 1569-1635. From Moyrath in Co. Meath,
he joined the Capuchins in Brussels. By continuous pressure, he
succeeded in persuading the General Chapter at Rome to erect an
Irish Capuchin Mission, with himself as commissary general, on
29th. May 1608. He started a school at Cologne, which was moved
to Lille in 1610 and finally to Charleville. There Friar Nugent erected
the real mother-house of the Irish Province in 1615. This same year
the first Capuchin was sent to Ireland: Fr Stephen Daly. He was soon
followed by Fr Laurence Nugent. Two more friars came in 1618.
During his first visit home, in 1624, Friar Nugent obtained the loan
of a house outside Newgate in Dublin and this became the first
canonical foundation. The other religious orders in the city were
bitterly opposed to the new arrivals. This situation continued for a

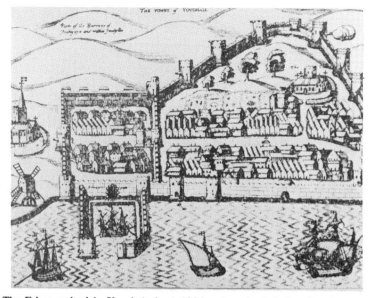

The Friars arrived in Youghal about 1226 and made their first foundation in Ireland there. This map shows the town of Youghal about the year 1600. Details of the Friary may be seen in the enlarged view below.
(from *Pacat'a Hibernia*).

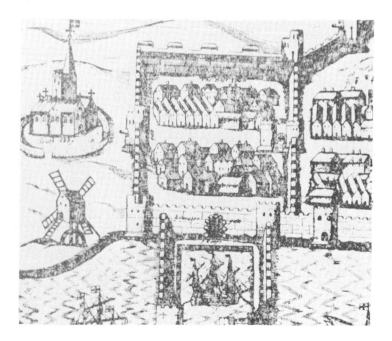

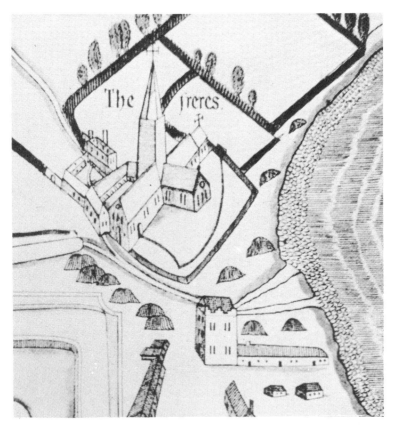

Carrickfergus Friary about 1540 (from UJA vii, 1859).

The last friary founded in Ireland — Rossnowlagh in Co. Donegal.

Rome: St Isidore's College. The Theological Hall with frescoes of Irish Franciscan scholars.

Prague: College of the Immaculate Conception as it was in the late eighteenth century. This was the largest Irish Franciscan Continental College.

Ross Abb

alway.

The Friary in Killarney about 1870, soon after it was built by the Belgian Franciscans.

Athlone Friary built in Hiberno-Romanesque style in 1930.

Carrickbeg: St Francis, eighteenth century folk art.

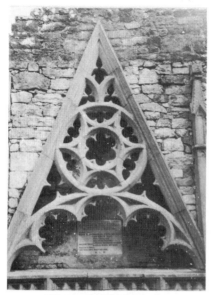

Kilconnell: O'Daly tomb.   **Kilconnell: anonymous tomb.**

Kilconnell, Co. Galway.

number of years and was not helped by the transfer of a number of Friars Minor to the Capuchins.

Given the climate of the times, it's not surprising that the number of foundations rose rapidly. By about 1642, there were some fifty-one friars on the mission in Ireland. In addition to Dublin, foundations had also been made at Cork, Drogheda, Limerick, Mullingar and Slane. Other houses were soon added at Athy, Clonmel, Galway, Swords and Thurles — although some of these were extremely small and may never have consisted of more than one or two friars. Like other religious, the Capuchins suffered greviously in the Cromwellian period. Many of their early foundations were lost, but the number of friars remained steady. In 1685 the house at Charleville was replaced by two others in France: Bar-sur-Aube and Vassy (in Champagne). Right up to their suppression in 1793, these two houses remained the back-bone of the Irish Capuchin Mission. The Provincial lived in France, the Chapters were held there, novices and students were trained there and in fact quite a number of friars never returned to Ireland. Some cynics remarked that the Irish Province was more French than Irish. There were only three foundations in Ireland during most of the eighteenth century, with about thirty Capuchins living in the country.

The Irish Capuchins had been erected into a Mission in 1608. This became a custody in 1698 and the Province of St Patrick was erected on 22nd. September 1733, with Fr Philip O'Kennedy as Minister Provincial. Efforts to extend the Irish Mission to Scotland and the Isle of Man failed towards the end of the seventeenth century.

As with other orders, the effects of the French Revolution were catastrophic for the Irish Capuchins, especially since they had been so strongly based in France. The rapid worsening of the situation in France resulted in the Irish Province being reduced to a General Commissariate in 1855. It became a custody in 1864 and was re-erected as a full province on 1st. November 1885. Since then the Capuchins have shared in the general growth of religious orders in Ireland during the first part of this present century and they continue to provide a very effective form of Franciscan witness.

2. The Second Order of St Francis — the Poor Clares

In most countries, the Second Order spread along with the First Order. Thus the first Poor Clare foundation in England was made at Northampton in 1252. Strangely, there is no solid evidence for the Second Order in Ireland until 1629. Such a community may have existed, especially following the Observant and Colettine reforms in the fifteenth century, but if it did, its records have faded from the pages of history.

Several Irish girls found their way to the Continent early in the seventeenth century and joined various Poor Clare convents. A number of English nuns had been able to set up an English Poor Clare Convent at Gravelines in 1607. This English foundation became a natural centre for Irish girls wishing to join the Order. The first known Irish Poor Clare is Sr Martha Marianna Cheevers, and she inspired a group of five nuns to establish an Irish Poor Clare convent at Dunkirk in 1625. This foundation was not a success. On the advice of the Irish Franciscans at Louvain, the nuns moved to Nieuport in 1627.

Under Mother Cecily of St Francis Dillon, the first group of Poor Clares arrived in Ireland in June 1629. The Franciscan friars, meeting in Chapter at Limerick in August, gave them an official welcome. Unfortunately the tolerant Lord Deputy, Falkland, had just been recalled and a mild persecution broke out. The sisters in Dublin, who had attracted some twelve postulants, were arrested on 22nd. October 1630.

Released on parole, they left Dublin and set up a convent at 'Bethlehem', where the ruins of their building may still be seen by the shores of Lough Ree some five miles north of Athlone. After ten years of rapid growth, the community numbered some sixty sisters. A new foundation was made at Drogheda in 1639. Bethlehem was sacked by an English army in May 1642. The community escaped. Some joined a small group of sisters who had gone to make a foundation in Galway in January 1642. Others escaped to Wexford, Waterford and Athlone.

On 10th. July 1649, Galway Corporation presented Nuns' Island to the Poor Clares. Forced to flee during the Cromwellian period, the sisters returned to Galway in 1660. Expelled in 1690, they set up their community in Market Sq. In 1825 they were able to return to Nuns' Island, where they have remained since.

All other Poor Clare communities in Ireland ceased to function during the various persecutions of the seventeenth century. In June 1712 a group of sisters set out from Galway to do social work in the Archdiocese of Dublin. After a long and complicated history, they eventually settled at Harold's Cross, where they founded an orphanage. From there a group went to found a school at Newry in May 1830. Newry became a centre for a series of foundations in Ulster. A national school was started at Cavan in 1861, from where a school was set up at Ballyjamesduff in 1872. From Newry, schools were also founded at 'Keady in 1871 and Mayobridge in 1922. Outside Ulster, a school was started at Kenmare in 1861, and the first Poor Clares arrived at Sydney, in Australia, in 1883.

The Poor Clares in Galway had long been anxious to return to a strictly contemplative life. Following a series of reforms, they returned to the strict observance of the 'Colettine' life on 16th. July 1892. The next year a group of Poor Clares from Levenshulme, near Manchester, under Mother Mary Seraphine Bowe, landed at Drogheda on their way to make a foundation at Carlow Graigue, at the invitation of the bishop, Dr Lynch. Conditions proved difficult and it took the sisters some time to settle in. In 1906, seven sisters were able to leave Carlow for a new foundation at Donnybrook, from where a group left to make a foundation at Belfast in 1924.

Sr Maria Dwyer of Cork had been professed at Tournai in Belgium. With the help of the bishop of Cork and of her father, she and another sister came to Cork where they made a new foundation on Christmas Day 1914. Four sisters came from Carlow to join them. As the community in Cork grew, plans were made for a foundation in Ennis. The first stone was laid on 17th. September 1957, and the sisters were able to leave Cork for their new home on 8th. November 1958. The Newry Poor Clares made foundations at Stanmullen in 1951 and at Gormanston in 1957.

Two converts from Anglicanism, Elizabeth Sophia Law and Mary Anne Hayes, were received into the Catholic Church in 1851. They, and another lady, went to Paris and became Franciscan Third Order Regular nuns. In 1854, following their return to London, they set up the congregation of the Franciscan Sisters of Perpetual Adoration. Life in England proved difficult and, with the help of the Ram family, the sisters came to Gorey in 1858. Again matters did not work out quite as expected, but eventually a community of nine settled into their final home at Drumshanbo, where the first Solemn Mass was sung on 8th. December 1864. A second, short-lived, foundation was made at Drumsna on 8th. August 1918.

Following the Second Vatican Council, it was suggested that a federation would be the best way of organising the Poor Clares in Ireland. Although all the Poor Clare convents belonged to the same observance, the fact that many of them were leading a life that was partly active and partly contemplative rather than strictly contemplative produced a movement towards two unified groups. On 14th. April 1973, the contemplatives formed a federation with Nuns' Island, Galway, as the Head House and including three English houses. In practice the main effort so far has gone into the drafting of common constitutions and the creation of a common system of formation. In August 1973, the Sisters of the Perpetual Adoration at Drumshanbo decided to become Poor Clares and join in the federation. The sisters of the Second Order who live a mixed life formed another federation, based on a system of provinces, on Ascension Thursday, 8th. May 1975. The head house of the Irish section is Newry.

3. Franciscan Third Order Regular (Medieval)

The ideals of the Franciscan Third Order Secular, when lived in full sincerity, have led many to embrace the religious life. In medieval times, groups of tertiaries began to come together to form regular communities. The concept of a proper religious congregation began to emerge in 1412 under Pope John XXIII. From decrees of Martin V in 1425 and 1426, there would seem to have been Third Order Regular communities in Ireland by that date. These were communities of men. There is some evidence for communities of women at a later date, but these never became very prominent and will not be discussed here.

The first foundation was probably at Killeenbrenan (near Shrule in Co. Mayo) before 1426, and the next at Clonkeenkerrill (East Galway) about 1435. These were rapidly followed by many foundations in the Gaelic areas in the West and North. The brothers seem to have depended on priests of the First Order for services at the start, but afterwards began to ordain some of their own members. The structure of the Third Order Regular was that of a loose federation. They were chiefly concerned with education, prayer and a life of Franciscan witness.

By 1450 the Third Order Regular had twelve houses. This number grew to thirty-six by 1500 and to forty at the time of the Suppression. With very few exceptions, they were concentrated in Ulster and West of the Shannon. Structurally these buildings vary from miniature First Order friaries (compare Rosserk with nearby Moyne) through a simple church with residence attached (Bonamargy, Clonkeenkerrill) to a tiny chapel and residence (Friarstown). Being comparatively late, most of the buildings are good examples of reticulated or flamboyant style. The casual observer will tend to confuse them with First Order buildings.

Since the houses of the Third Order were usually in isolated areas, they managed to weather the first stages of the Reformation fairly well. About twelve communities survived the Elizabethan persecutiohs. Most of these were in mid-Ulster and enjoyed protection by the local chiefs. After the Flight of the Earls, the fate of these houses was sealed. They were slowly suppressed and thus the history of the Third Order Regular in medieval Ireland draws to a close about 1620.

4. Franciscan Third Order Regular (Modern)

About 1817, a group of zealous men, members of the Third Order Secular attached to Merchant's Quay Friary, Dublin, came together and took religious vows. Their director was Fr John (Francis) Dunne ofm. They soon opened three schools to educate the poor — one at Milltown, and two in Dalkey (Co. Dublin).

In 1818 Christopher Dillon Bellew, with the approval of Dr Kelly, archbishop of Tuam, invited the brothers to open a school at Mountbellew. They came, although the foundation stone of a permanent building was not laid until 1823. The schools near Dublin were eventually closed and the official name of the new congregation became 'The Franciscan Brothers of the Third Order Regular, Mountbellew'. They remained under the control of the First Order until the passing of Catholic Emancipation in 1829. Taking fright at the severe anti-religious parts of this Bill, they petitioned the Holy See to be placed under the jurisdiction of the Archbishop of Tuam. This was granted in 1830 and, under the protection of Dr MacHale, they began to expand rapidly in the West, hence their popular name — Monks of the West.

Mountbellew became the base for expansion to such places as Clifden, Roundstone, Errew, Tourmakeady, Achill, Cummer, Granlahan, Kilkerrin and Annadown. Another Franciscan group started at Clara, from where a foundation was made, in conjunction with Mountbellew, at Farragher. This loose federation was united by decree of Benedict XV on 5th. February 1918 and was erected into a full Pontifical Brotherhood on 21st. June 1938. At present, in addition to houses at eight places in Ireland, the brothers have three houses in the U.S.A. and two each in both Nigeria and the Cameroon.

5. Franciscan Sisterhoods

It would be impossible to deal comprehensively with the female counterpart of the Franciscan brothers in such a work as this. I would have to discuss such an item as the influence of Fr Lawrence Callanan ofm. on Nano Nagle, foundress of the Presentation Sisters, or provide a complete list of all the congregations in Ireland which are in some way associated with the Franciscan rule of life and spirit. There is a vast number of institutes which use the rule of the Third Order as a basis for their life. The following are the more important in Ireland.

— The Franciscan Missionaries of Mary were founded in Madras (India) by Mother Mary of the Passion in 1877 and have an Irish house at Loughglynn, Co. Roscommon.

— The Franciscan Missionaries of the Divine Motherhood started officially in 1935 when the late Mother Mary Francis Spring, who had joined another congregation in 1918, led a group to found Mount Alverna Nursing Home at Guilford in England. Final papal approval was received in 1963. In Ireland their main

69

foundation is the Portiuncula Hospital, Ballinasloe, with others at Waterford and Beaufort (Co. Kerry).

— The Franciscan Missionary Sisters of St Joseph have houses at Farranferris (Cork) and Freshford (Co. Kilkenny). They were founded at Mill Hill, London, in 1883 by Mother Mary Francis Ingham, with the help of Cardinal Vaughan.

— The Franciscan Missionary Sisters for Africa have their Generalate at Mount Oliver, Dundalk. Going back to 1903, their first Superior General was Mother Mary Kevin, 'Mama Kevina'.

— The Franciscan Missionaries of Our Lady (up to 1965, Franciscan Sisters of Calais) run the Honan Home in Cork and the Sacred Heart Hospital, Ballinderry. These sisters came into existence through an amalgamation of several Third Order houses in France in 1854.

— The Franciscan Sisters of the Atonement, the female side of the Graymoor Friars, run a hostel for the elderly at Rossinver in Co. Leitrim.

— The Sisters of the Third Order Regular of St Francis, founded by ex-Anglicans in 1868, have a foundation near Castleblaney in Co. Monaghan.

— The Franciscan Sisters of the Immaculate Conception run a school at Falcarragh in Co. Donegal.

— The Missionary Franciscan Sisters of the Immaculate Conception were founded by Mother Mary Ignatius Hayes at Belle Prairie in the U.S.A in 1873 and their main Irish house was at Bloomfield, Co. Westmeath.

— The Franciscan Sisters of Glen Riddle had a foundation in Mallow until recently.

— The Sisters of the Holy Cross in Belfast, founded in Switzerland in 1844, are also connected with the Franciscan family.

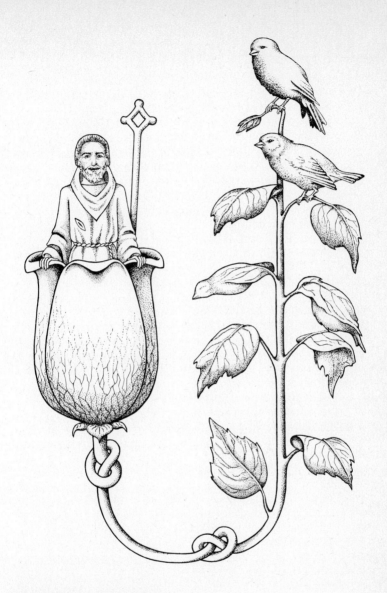

When St Francis talked of Christ . . .
. . . all of creation, even the birds, had to listen,
yet the beauty of the world . . .
. . . talked to Francis of the hand of the Creator.

(Dromahair Friary, c. 1530.)

71

Appendix

IRISH FRANCISCAN SITES

There are three types of Irish Franciscan sites: medieval sites where there are still traces of large stone buildings, small houses or cottages used as places of refuge or for parish work during the Penal period, and modern friaries. From an architectural view-point, we may neglect the latter two classes, even though some of the buildings may be extremely interesting for the historian. Most modern friaries are revival style buildings from the second half of the last century. Quite often there is nothing to distinguish the small houses used for parish work from the ordinary residences of people of those times. These buildings were just simply a normal country cottage.

The medieval friary was a complex building. A narrow church ran east-west. The main altar was at the eastern end, under a huge and ornate East Window. This window was both practical, in that it admitted the light of the rising sun, and symbolical, in that the rising sun was a sign of the Risen Christ. This eastern end of the church served as a choir for the friars, while the western end was a nave for the people. The pillars supporting a tall, slender tower divided choir from nave. Between these pillars was a small loft, usually of wood, known as the rood loft. This served as a pulpit for preaching. The friars often built a small transept chapel, usually containing two altars, to the south of the junction of tower and nave. In a few cases, an aisle was added to the south of the nave itself.

Artistically, the most important feature of the church was the East Window. Window design underwent a continuous evolution from the thirteenth century single lancets, through the thirteenth and fourteenth century grouped lancets, through fourteenth century windows of many lights, on to the switch, or switch and bar, tracery of the fifteenth century, and ending with the reticulated, or flamboyant, tracery of the sixteenth century. The choir was often the site of several important tombs, traces of which may still remain. Other interesting pieces of sculpture may be found around the main windows, both inside and out, and on corbels and finials, especially underneath the tower.

The residential part of the friary usually consisted of three ranges gathered around a cloister on the north side of the church. The east range normally contained the sacristy and refectory, while the north range enclosed the kitchen area. The dormitories, typified by small narrow windows, were usually on the first floor over the kitchen and the refectory, so that the heat from these rooms would help to keep

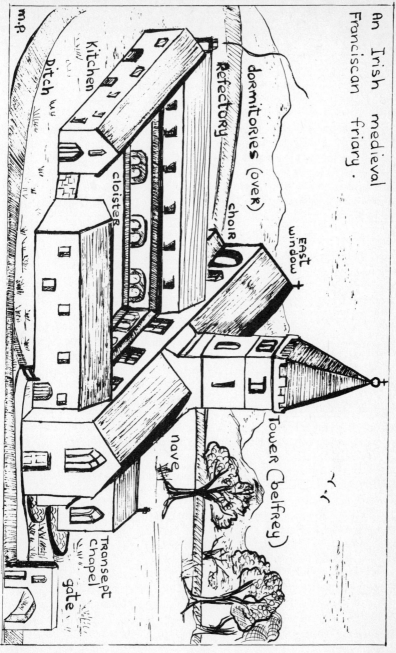

An Irish medieval Franciscan friary.

m.p.
Ditch
Kitchen
cloister
Refectory
dormitories (over)
choir
EAST window
Tower (belfrey)
nave
Transept chapel
gate

73

the sleeping area warm. The west range consisted of various store-rooms and workshops. The three ranges were normally connected by an ambulatory — the covered walk around the central garden area, often called 'the cloisters'. In early friaries the arcade of the ambulatory was usually free-standing, but in later friaries it often bears the wall of the dormitory. There is nearly always some trace of a stream flowing by the north range, both to supply fresh water and to take away sewage.

These central buildings were surrounded by a series of outhouses, workshops etc. The whole area was entered through a gate with a niche for the patron saint. Where water was plentiful, there was always a mill, and in many cases a weir as well. There are very few places today where one can see all these buildings, but often one can close one's eyes and imagine the brown-clad friars moving around the various parts of the friary, while a bell tolled out from the tall tower which dominated the whole complex.

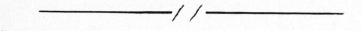

NOTE ON WINDOWS

WINDOW STYLES, especially of the East Window, evolved during the medieval period, starting with *(a) lancets*, in groups of three or five (still standing at Waterford c. 1250, Nenagh c. 1260, and Ardfert c. 1265; traces remain behind the altered windows at Claregalway c. 1260 and Buttevant c. 1275; believed to have existed at Cashel c. 1265, Clonmel c. 1270 and Carrickbeg 1336). Ennis c. 1300 provides a unique example *(b)* of the *transition* to *(c)* windows of many *lights* (Timoleague c. 1305 and the beautiful seven light window at Kilkenny 1321). After a gap of about a century, two styles emerged almost simultaneously: *(e) switch tracery* (e.g. Askeaton c. 1430, Muckross c. 1440 and Adare c. 1465) and *(d) switch and bar tracery* (e.g. Quin c. 1430, Claregalway c. 1435 and Ross c. 1470). Towards the end of the fifteenth century, the imagination of the architects began to change the tracery, giving rise to *(f)* tentative *experiments* (Moyne c. 1470, also Buttevant c. 1480, but of a different type). The culmination of three centuries of evolution were *(g)* the beautiful *flamboyant* windows (still standing at Meelick c. 1445, Lislaughlin c. 1470, Kilconnell c. 1500 and Dromahair 1508; also the South Window at Multyfarnham; known to have existed at Roscrea c. 1470 and Donegal c. 1475), as well as *(h) reticulated* windows (not common in Franciscan friaries, except for choir window at Buttevant c. 1480 and the West Window at Dromahair c. 1510).

Evolution of window styles:

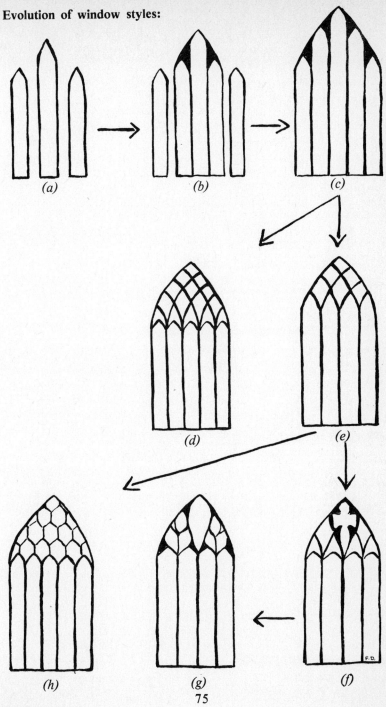

(a)   *(b)*   *(c)*

(d)   *(e)*

(h)   *(g)*   *(f)*

Nenagh Friary

Kilkenny Friary

Muckross Friary

76

SITES IN IRELAND

ADARE (Co. Limerick)
Site at the far end of the golf course, or through the Dunraven Estate.
Remains: church complete with tower and transept chapel; large sections of the convent and cloister; old gateway and some outbuildings; N.B. — a bas relief of St Francis in the cloister, traces of flower patterns on the top right tomb in the choir — at least two wooden statues are known to exist.

Begun in 1464 and dedicated to St Michael two years later, Adare friary was one of the first Observant foundations, and was built by order of Thomas FitzGerald, Earl of Kildare. The friars were able to remain until about 1578. They returned in 1633 and remained, except for a brief period during the Cromwellian persecution, until the middle of the following century.

ARAN (Inishmore, Co. Galway)
Site near St Eany's Round Tower in Killeany.
Remains: nothing substantial, since the stones were used to build Arkin's Castle in 1587.

Probably begun in 1485 for the Conventual friars, Aran friary seems to have died with the arrival of Sir John Rawson about the year 1587. Weak efforts to restore the friary about 1640 were unsuccessful.

ARDFERT (Co. Kerry)
Site in fields about a mile north-east of the village and the cathedral.
Remains: the church and transept chapel are complete, as is the tower, which is situated in an unusual position; a small section of the convent still stands, with the cloister; the friary church should be visited in conjunction with the almost identical cathedral.

The friars were invited to the area by Thomas FitzMaurice about the year 1253. It remained a Conventual foundation to about 1517 and was taken over as a barracks in 1584. The friars returned in 1613, after which they came and went as circumstances permitted throughout the rest of that century and afterwards until at least as late as 1763.

ARMAGH (city)
Site just inside the gate of the residence of the Anglican Archbishop.
Remains: three walls of the church, part of the transept chapel, all recently excavated.

There were friars in Armagh as early as 1241, but the permanent foundation there dates to 1263-4 and Archbishop Maol Padraig Ó Sgannail op. It's likely that the friars left their old house when the

77

English took over the city in 1551, but they certainly remained in hiding within the city. They were found and flogged in 1587. Places of refuge were situated at Brantry (Tyrone) and Creggan (Armagh). For later history, see under Dungannon.

ASKEATON (Co. Limerick)
Site on the east bank of the river, just north of the village.
Remains: church and transept chapel complete, but tower has fallen; convent and cloisters complete on the south side of the church (exceptional), with an excellent refectory added later; traces of the boundary wall and outbuildings: N.B. — the bas relief of St Francis in the north-east corner of the cloister, many masons' marks, the tomb of the unknown pilgrim, bas relief of unknown bishop in the choir, excellent reader's desk in the refectory; wooden statue exists.

Probably founded by Gerald 'The Poet', fourth Earl of Desmond, about the year 1400, but the present friary buildings date to slightly later. The community became Observant in 1497 and escaped suppression until about 1579, when the building was sacked by Nicholas Malby and several friars were killed. Some managed to remain on in the area and were able to return to the old building in 1627. There is evidence that the community remained active down to about the year 1740. Even after this date, some of the friars were acting as curates in Glin as late as 1766.

ATHLONE (Co. Westmeath)
The medieval site was near the present Abbey graveyard, and all later sites were in the area of the present friary.
Remains: the remaining stones of the medieval building were used in the foundations of the present church; the ruins at Abbey Road are those of a church begun about 1660 and which may never have been used.

The friary church in Athlone was consecrated in 1241. Charles de Burgo was the main founder. The building was badly damaged by a malicious fire in 1398. With the coming of the Reformation, the friars drifted into obscurity. They were certainly active again in 1627, when they returned to the town. They erected a small house at Killinure soon after. The community numbered eighteen by the time of their expulsion from the town in 1651, but they remained near at hand, as is shown by the death of Br John O'Claffey, killed in 1653. After the Restoration, the friars began to build at Abbey Road, but seem to have abandoned this site fairly soon. By about 1730 we find them at their present site, where they built a new chapel in 1819. In the meanwhile, many of them had worked in the diocese as parish clergy during the eighteenth century, not only in Athlone itself, but also in such places as Ballinahown and Clonmacnoise. Work started on a new friary in 1869 and a school, St Bonaventure's Academy, was opened in 1871. The foundation stone of the present church, built in an idealised Hiberno-Romanesque style, was laid in 1930.

BALLINABARNY (Co. Wicklow)
The site is near the Glen of Imail.

There was a friary here for a number of years in the 1640's.

BALLINASAGGART (Co. Longford)
The site is just south-west of Edgeworthstown and there are no major remains.

The friary of St John the Baptist of Longford began life as a Third Order Regular friary in the fifteenth century. The First Order got permission to take it over in 1635. The friary was plundered by the Earl of Westmeath in 1651, but the friars had returned to the area by 1658. As late as 1801 there were still four friars there. The end probably came with the death of Fr Thomas McCormick in 1811.

BALLYMOTE (Co. Sligo)
The site is near the present Catholic Church.
Remains: almost complete church, with traces of the convent.

A Third Order friary, founded in 1442, was taken over by the First Order about 1643. The friars used the site for about a hundred years after this.

BANTRY (Co. Cork)
The site was the present Abbey graveyard, where some of the stones belonging to the friary have been gathered together. There is one carved head among these.

Founded by an O'Sullivan or an O'Mahoney, Bantry friary became Observant in 1482 after twenty years of Conventual rule. The building was pulled down by Domhnall O'Sullivan Beare in 1559 to prevent the English from using it. Individual friars remained in the area, especially at Cape Clear, until the middle of the eighteenth century.

BONAMARGY (Co. Antrim)
The site is just off the A2, beside Ballycastle Golf Club.
Remains: a small church, the transept chapel of which has been turned into the burial vault of the Earls of Antrim; also parts of the convent and outhouses.

Founded for the Third Order Regular about 1500, the friary was burned by the Irish and Scots in 1584 while it was being used by the English army. About 1626 it was taken over by the First Order and used as a base for the Scottish Mission (cf. Chapter 5) until 1647. The friars occasionally returned to the site afterwards, either with the aim of re-opening the Scottish Mission, or in connection with parish work, which continued down to the death of Fr Michael McMullin in 1789.

BUTTEVANT (Co. Cork)

The site is on the main street beside the present Catholic Church. **Remains:** the church and transept are complete, but the tower has fallen; many stones belonging to the cloister arcade are stored in the upper vault under the choir, while there are good carved stones in the lower vault; note the re-building of various windows in the church.

Dedicated to St Thomas à Becket, the friary was founded by the de Barry family, certainly by 1276, possibly by 1251. The de Barrys also protected the friars following the Reformation, so that the friars remained working in the area right up to the Cromwellian period. The friars returned at the Restoration, and there were at least two of them in residence during the eighteenth century. By 1800, there was only one old friar left, and he died soon afterwards.

CARRICKBEG (Co. Waterford)

The remains of the old friary have been incorporated into the present parish church across the road from the present friary; N.B. — the unusual tower, riding on the church wall, and the carved figures around the church door.

The first superior of Carrickbeg friary, John Clynn, has left us his annals, so we can state that it was founded in 1336 by James Butler, Earl of Desmond. It was an early victim of the Suppression and was vacant for nearly a hundred years until the friars returned to the area in 1644. Soon expelled by the Cromwellians, the friars returned in 1669. They built a thatched house, and later a thatched chapel, in the grounds of the present friary. Following an 'accident' a proper church was built in 1822 and extended in 1839-49. The convent was added in 1896.

CARRICKFERGUS (Co. Antrim)

The site is just off Joymount St. There are no remains, but the area is under excavation at present (1976-7).

An early Franciscan foundation in Ireland, it received a royal grant in 1248. The Observant reform was introduced from Donegal in 1497. Early suppressed, it was used as a munitions store until it was re-built as Joymount House by Sir Arthur Chichester in 1618. From 1626 on, the friars made several attempts to return to the area, but were never successful. Occasional parish work was carried on there by the friars in the eighteenth century.

CASHEL (Co. Tipperary)

The present Catholic parish church is on the site of the medieval friary.
Remains: while nothing remains of the buildings, some pieces of cut

stone and some carvings are kept in the Presentation Convent graveyard; a sarcophagus is used as a font in the parish church; N.B. — four tomb slabs (a knight and three ladies) have been inserted into the walls around the Church of Ireland cathedral.

'Hacket's Abbey' was founded by Sir William Hacket about 1265. It later became the head-house of one of the custodies of the Irish Franciscan Province. Despite the fact that the Anglican archbishop got possession of the friary at the Suppression, the friars were able to remain on until about 1550. One famous friar in Cashel at this period was the notorious Myler Magrath (cf. Chapter 4). The friars returned to Cashel in 1618, but left after the sacking of the town by Lord Inchiquin in 1647. The friars were back by 1658 and remained on until the eighteenth century. For later history, see under Thurles.

CASTLEDERMOT (Co. Kildare)
The site is just outside the town on the Carlow road.
Remains: the church is complete with a large transept chapel and an unusual tower; the three small chapels within the transept chapel are much admired.

Certainly founded before 1247, Castledermot friary was practically re-founded by Thomas, Lord of Ossory, when he gave a substantial building grant in 1302. Situated on the edge of the Pale, it was still in Conventual hands when it was one of the first friaries to be suppressed, in 1540. The Observant friars did not return to the area until 1639, and were soon expelled by the Cromwellians. Back in 1661, the friars maintained a presence in the area until the middle of the eighteenth century.

CASTLELYONS (Co. Cork)
While the main foundation here was Carmelite, there is vague evidence for a Franciscan residence in the region early in the eighteenth century.

CAVAN (town)
The site was that of the present graveyard in Abbey St.
Remains: the tower is complete, but in a much altered condition.

The town of Cavan grew up around the friary founded, according to tradition, by Giolla-Íosa O'Reilly, Lord of Breffny, about 1300. The friary was burned by the English in 1468. After the community adopted the Observant reform, many of them were drowned in a boating accident in 1516. Despite the Suppression, the friars were able to remain on until 1608. They returned in 1616, but community life slowly became impossible. The remaining friars began to act as parish clergy. There were seven Franciscans working in the area in 1800, and still two in 1820, of whom the last died in 1826.

CLANE (Co. Kildare)

The site is in the graveyard on the Naas road, just after leaving the village.

Remains: large sections of the church and transept walls; damaged effigy of a knight.

The effigy is said to be that of Gerald FitzMaurice FitzGerald, who is reputed to have founded the friary in 1258. Having undergone major re-building in 1433, the friary was suppressed in 1540 and a lot of the stone used in the repair of Maynooth castle. The friars never really returned to the area, except for a couple of years after 1647, and there are very few records of friars engaged in parish work in the region.

CLAREGALWAY (Co. Galway)

The site is to the west of the village, on the main Galway-Tuam road.

Remains: these are much more extensive than the visitor might believe at a first glance, since the modern entrance is from the back of the old building; the church, tower, large sections of the transept and aisle are almost complete; a large part of the convent still stands, but on the south, or exceptional, side of the church; traces of outbuildings and the original gateway into the friary are in evidence.

John de Cogan, who also founded the Carthusian house at Kilnalahan (see below), invited the friars to Claregalway about 1250. One of the largest friaries in the country, it remained Conventual right up to the time of its Suppression under Henry VIII. The friars managed to remain on until 1589. It was only in 1641 that a regular community was re-established there. Expelled by the Cromwellians, the friars returned after the Restoration. There was a community of five living in the old friary in 1766, and four in 1801. At some time during the 1850's, the remaining community withdrew to Galway city, but travelled out regularly to say mass in Claregalway over a period of about twenty years. Tradition has it that Fr John (Anthony) Francis was the last resident friar in Claregalway. He died in 1858.

CLONKEENKERRILL (Co. Galway)

The site is in an isolated graveyard about four miles north of Attymon.

Remains: most of the church and transept chapel.

About 1435, the bishop of Clonfert gave permission to two brothers, David and John Mulkerrill, to convert the old parish church into a Third Order friary. In 1453 permission was obtained to change to the First Order. The friary seems to have escaped suppression, since it was still occupied in 1618. It was abandoned soon afterwards.

CLONMEL (Co. Tipperary)

The medieval site was that of the present friary church.

Remains: the tower and part of the choir wall are incorporated into the present church; N.B. — the tomb of the Barons of Cahir and associated sculptures, including an early trades-man's tomb-stone and a stone baptismal font.

Founded in 1269, probably by Sir Otho de Grandison, the friary became Observant in 1536, four years before it was suppressed. The friars remained on in the town and were able to open an official residence in 1616. After the Restoration, we find them living in Irishtown. During the eighteenth century, they helped the parish clergy in the parish church. Having obtained the old friary once again, they were able to re-open it for Catholic worship in 1828. The friars had a small school from 1873 to 1881. The church proved too small, so the present church was built, in what the architect believed was Early English style, and formally opened in 1886. Since then, the friary residence has been added (in 1891-92) and a small St Anthony Chapel built (1959).

CORK (city)

There are no remains of the medieval friary at the site on the North Mall.

After the friars landed at Youghal, they probably made their first permanent foundation in Cork about 1230. The city was the scene of a notorious Provincial Chapter in 1291 (see Chapter 1). Late to adopt the Observant reform (about 1500), it was one of the first friaries to be suppressed. The friars lived on in hiding and there was a community of nine in their place of refuge in 1615. After the Restoration, the friars lived in a thatched cottage in Shandon and worked quite openly until the Penal period. They then moved through a number of hiding places, e.g. in Cotner's Lane, before settling in the present Broad Lane area sometime before 1759. A new friary was opened in 1813, following which the Franciscan novitiate was transferred to Cork for a number of years. Problems arose between the friars and the bishop of Cork. These, and the fears that the religious orders in Ireland were about to be suppressed, delayed the building of a new church, which was not opened until 1829. A student hostel called St Anthony's Hall was opened in 1909 but had to close after a number of years. By 1881 both friary and church were considered unsafe, but it was not until 14th. July 1953 that the present church was opened and blessed, soon to be followed by the new friary.

83

COURTOWN (Co. Meath)

The cottage used by the friars as their residence was still standing some years ago.

When the friary inTrim came near to closing about 1700, the friars became involved in parish work in an area north of the town and also in an area around Navan. From an official residence at Courtown, they served the parishes of Bective, Clonmaduff, Courtown, Kilcooley, Moymet, Rataine and Tullaghenoge. They also worked for some time in the parishes of Donaghmore, Donaghpatrick, Kilberry and Loghan. In 1801 there was a community of three at Courtown, and a parish priest plus six curates working in the area — a total of ten. Courtown officially closed following the death of Fr Patrick Ryan in 1826.

CURRAHEEN (Aglish, Co. Waterford)

The last official residence of the friars, a two storey house, still stands.

Youghal was the first friary in Ireland. Persecution forced the friars across the river into Co. Waterford in the seventeenth century, but they retained the privileged title of Youghal. Soon after the Williamite period, certainly before 1739, the friars transferred the Youghal foundation to Curraheen and served in the church at Aglish. The surviving residence was built about 1845, but the last friar of Youghal, Fr P. D. Lonergan, died at Curraheen in 1862.

DERRY (city)

The presence of the friars in Derry is an enigma. There is evidence for a small residence there from 1687 on, and a strong local tradition of a Franciscan presence in the Waterside and Ardmore areas. The only friar associated with the city was Fr Francis Gallagher, who taught in the seminary there before his death in 1806. Despite the lack of an official connection, Derry has been a great source of vocations for the Order.

DERRYNAFLAN (Co. Tipperary)

There are remains of a medieval church on an island in the Bog of Lurgoe.

Another rather mysterious friary, this name appears in official documents from 1676 to 1724. The actual identification of the site is doubtful, but this island in the middle of a bog seems a likely place due to its associations with Cashel.

DONEGAL (town)

The site is in a graveyard just beyond the harbour.
Remains: parts of the choir, transept chapel and cloisters.

Despite its fame, Donegal friary was a rather late foundation, by

Nuala O'Connor and her son, the first Red Hugh O'Donnell, for the Observant friars in 1473-4. It was damaged by an accidental fire in 1536. Under Irish protection, it escaped suppression until raided by the English in 1588, who then occupied it as a fort. They were expelled by THE Red Hugh O'Donnel, whose brother-in-law, Niall Garbh, later seized it for the English again. On the morning of the 20th. September 1601, the building was almost destroyed when the gun-powder stored in it exploded. Efforts to re-build it for the friars ended after the Flight of the Earls. The friars went to live by the banks of the river Drowes, the scene of much of the work on the *Annals of the Four Masters*. Individual friars worked in Donegal down to the middle of the last century, and the late Cardinal Logue, who was born in 1840, claimed that he had been baptised by a wandering friar in S. Donegal!

DOWNPATRICK (town)

There are now no major remains on the presumed site, that of the courthouse.

We are inclined to forget that Downpatrick was one of the two major towns in the Earldom of Ulster and we should not be surprised that the Earl himself, Hugh de Lacy, brought the friars there about 1235. It was burned by Bruce in 1316. An Anglo-Irish foundation, Downpatrick friary remained Conventual right up to the Reformation. Despite oppression, the friars remained on until three were killed by an English force in 1575. Observant friars returned to the town in 1627 and remained until the Cromwellian period. For later history, see under Dromore.

DROGHEDA (Co. Louth)

Nothing remains of the early friary, situated between the Laurence Gate and the river.

Drogheda friary was founded about 1240, but the exact details are uncertain. In 1330 the building was badly damaged by flooding, and, in 1349, twenty five members of the community died during the Black Death. The community did not become Observant until 1506. Suppressed in 1540, it was abandoned about five years later. Some friars did continue to visit the city, since one was arrested for saying mass there in 1607, but a formal community was not re-established until 1610. During the seventeenth and eighteenth centuries the friars came and went as circumstances permitted. In 1798 they purchased an old store for conversion into a chapel, but work could not begin until 1829. First mass was celebrated there on 22nd. August 1830. Extensions were undertaken in 1835 and again in 1842. Drogheda friary became a favoured house within the Irish Province, and the

85

novitiate was there from 1860 to 1877. There is also some evidence for a friary school at Drogheda. The Brown, or reform, friars took over in 1923.

DROMAHAIR (Creevelea Friary, Co. Leitrim)

The friary of Creevelea is in a graveyard about a ten minute walk through a wooded area from Dromahair village.

Remains: a church with transept chapel and tower (altered); large sections of the convent and cloister; N.B. — an immense amout of good stone-work: the flamboyant east and west windows in the church, reliefs on the mullions of the east window, animal motifs under the tower, and especially two bas-reliefs of St Francis on the side of a pillar in the cloister, one of St Francis preaching to the birds, the other of the Stigmata of St Francis.

Observant friars from Donegal were invited in 1508 by Margaret O'Brien and her husband, Eoghan O'Rourke, to make this foundation, the last pre-Reformation Franciscan foundation in Ireland. Before it was completed, the buildings were badly damaged by an accidental fire in 1536. The friary escaped suppression until it was occupied as a barracks by Sir Richard Bingham in 1590. It was 1618 before the friars were able to set up a permanent residence again. As usual, the friars had to depart during Cromwellian times, but returned after the Restoration. They then became involved in parish work in the area. The last friar of Dromahair was Fr Peter Magauran, who died in 1837.

DROMORE (Co. Down)

The exact site is uncertain and there are no major remains.

A residence was set up in Dromore following the Provincial Chapter of 1637 in order to relieve pressure on the friars of Downpatrick. Despite evidence that they abandoned the area about 1717, the friars continued to work there. They set up a school at Drumnacoile, which was eventually handed over to lay teachers. Only one priest was still alive in 1796, having spent a life-time serving the local·chapel. He died before 1800.

DUBLIN (city)

The site of the medieval friary was that of the catholic church in Francis St. There are no remains and all later sites were in the Cook St area.

It would seem that a group of friars travelled to Dublin fairly soon after their initial landing at Youghal. The early history of Dublin friary is obscure. Some authorities suggest that the friars tried a number of sites before settling in Francis St. Henry III was a notable benefactor, if not the actual founder. At least twenty three friars died

86

there during the Black Death. An Anglo-Irish foundation, Dublin friary did not accept the Observant reform until 1521. It was an early target for suppression, but the community were able to continue in existence until 1543.

While individual friars may have continued in the city, it was not until 1615 that a community returned and took up residence in Cook St. Following a raid on 26th. December 1629, they had to find another house in the same area. Expelled by the Cromwellians, the friars returned at the Restoration and tried to resume residence at their old site in Francis St. The little chapel they erected there served as the pro-Cathedral of Dublin until it was replaced by the present church of St Nicholas in 1834.

In the meantime, the friars had returned to Cook St, where their church was in such a bad state of repair that it literally collapsed. A new chapel was opened in 1749, almost back to back with the parish church of St Michael. In 1766 there were nine friars in the community, with another three on parish work in other parts of the city. By this time the friars had obtained a small house on Merchant's Quay. To disguise the chapel, the entrance was through the *Adam and Eve Inn*, thus the popular name of the present church and friary.

The old church of St Michael was purchased in 1815. The foundation stone of a new church and friary was laid on 16th. April 1834. The architect was Patrick Byrne. Given the limited resources of the times, the original plan took over a century to complete and the church was not consecrated until 29th. April 1939, by which time apse, dome, aisles, facade and shrines had been added to the original building. As part of the re-organisation of the central Dublin parishes, the Church of the Immaculate Conception, Merchant's Quay, to use the official title, became parish church of a new parish in 1974.

Note: friars teaching in the technical schools have a house in Mountjoy St since 1975. Broc House in Nutley Lane served as a university residence run by the Irish Franciscans since 1971. Ballywaltrim, near Bray, became a Franciscan parish in 1976.

DUNDALK (Co. Louth)
The site is in Seatown.
Remains: the tower, unusual in that it stood at the end of the aisle; a baptismal font in St Nicholas is reputed to have come from the friary.

Founded before 1246, Dundalk friary owed its origins to the de Verdon family. Some twenty three friars were killed when it was burned by Bruce in 1315. It was still a Conventual house when it was seized in 1539 by order of Sir Leonard Grey. The friars went to live in a small cottage and they adopted the Observant reform in 1556, just before they were driven out in 1563. The friars returned officially in 1626, when they had a dispute with the Carmelites over priorities.

A similar dispute after the Restoration, this time with the Dominicans, involved the Primate, St Oliver Plunkett. Although there was a community of seven in 1731, the friars left the town in the following year. They continued to work in neighbouring country parishes, especially at Creggan in S. Armagh, where one of them was still working as a curate as late as 1801.

DUNGANNON (Co. Tyrone)
There are traces of a house and church near the top of Drumbeam Hill.

Dungannon friary was started in 1687, on the basis of a fifteenth century Third Order foundation, to relieve pressure on Armagh. Eventually the two communities were united into one and settled near Donaghmore where there were seven friars in 1766. Inevitably the friars became involved in parish work and the last friar, Fr Francis O'Neill, died as acting parish priest in 1816-7.

ELPHIN (Co. Roscommon)
The site was at the eastern end of the village, but there are no significant remains.

One Cornelius, Bishop of Elphin, granted the old church of St Patrick to the friars before 1450. The old Irish monastery of St Patrick had been given to the Canons Regular of St Augustine about 1140, but the church had ceased to be the cathedral of the diocese in 1244. The Canons Regular seem to have died out about 1440. The friars were expelled by the Anglican bishop in 1563. The Observant friars were unable to return until 1632. Expelled by the Cromwellians from their old friary, which had been converted into the Anglican bishop's residence, the friars shipped some of their valuables to Louvain in 1654! They returned again in 1658 and the community grew to a total of nine in 1766. The second last friar in the community went to Rome in 1787, leaving one old bed-ridden friar behind. Soon after, the parish priest of Castlereagh paid for the education of a number of friars from the area in the hope of restoring Elphin friary. One of these, Fr Edward Garraghan, who was Minister Provincial in 1815-9, worked near Elphin for most of his life until he died in 1835.

ENNIS (Co. Clare)
The old friary is situated just around the corner from the present one.
Remains: church, tower and transept chapel are complete, as are the east range and parts of the cloister; N.B. — the tremendous amount of cut stone and bas-reliefs: the MacMahon tomb in its original form and the parts incorporated into another tomb, St Francis, the small Ecce Homo, and all the stone work under the tower.

The old tradition is that Donnach O'Brien founded Ennis friary on an island near his castle and that the town grew up around both. Be that as it may, construction had started before the death of Donnach in 1242. Later Ennis friary became a famous centre of learning. It would seen that it was slow to accept the Observant reform. The house was suppressed in 1543, but the community managed to remain on until 1575. Individual friars still remained, such as 'The Mad Friar', Fr Dermot O'Brien, who was certified insane so that he could live within the town about the year 1617. A small community was established in the area in 1627 and, with the usual interruption in the Cromwellian period, lasted right down to the next century. During the Cromwellian period the friars seem to have had places of refuge at Doolough Lake and Inagh. Following the Decree for the Expulsion of Religious, at least four friars registered as parish clergy, while others continued to live as best they could. By 1800 they were living as a community in Lysaght's Lane, and they managed to open a new chapel and friary at Bow Lane on 12th. December 1830. Following a threat by the Provincial in 1853 that he would close Ennis friary unless conditions were improved, the present site at Willow Bank House was obtained and the first mass was celebrated in the new church there on 1st. January 1856. Twenty years later this building was replaced by the present church. Ennis became the official novitiate of the Irish Province from 1876 to 1902, but the history of the novitiate during this period is complex (see Chapter 8). The old medieval friary was returned to the friars as an ecumental gesture by the Church of Ireland in 1969.

ENNISCORTHY (Co. Wexford)
The site was just off the present Abbey Square.
Remains: most of the stones were used to build the catholic cathedral in the last century; an old doorway belonging to the friary is still preserved at Lett's Brewery.

Founded in 1460, probably for the Observants, by a Cavanagh, little is known of the history of Enniscorthy friary before its suppression in 1540. The friars remained on and three of them were killed when the friary was plundered by Sir Henry Wallop in 1582. The rest of the community had dispersed by the end of the century. The friars returned between 1642 and 1650, and again from 1661 on. By 1688 they were involved in parish work and the history of the friary fades into obscurity towards 1750.

GALBALLY (Moor Abbey, Co. Tipperary)
The site is about a mile to the east of the village.
Remains: the church and tower are complete, but nothing remains of the convent.

Galbally was a late Conventual foundation, begun in 1471. After its suppression in 1540, the new owner, the Earl of Desmond, left the friars in peace until Sir Humphrey Gilbert burned the building in 1569, and Sir Henry Sidney again in 1570. The friars did not return until 1645. Expelled by the Cromwellians, they were back in 1658 and remained (with a short break during 1680-4) until 1748. Following a rather complicated dispute with Fr James Butler, V.G. of Cashel diocese, the friars of Galbally withdrew across the mountains to Mitchelstown, where the last friar of Galbally community died, probably in 1804.

GALWAY ABBEY (city)

The medieval friary was on St Stephen's Island, where the courthouse is now.

Remains: there are no substantial remains of the buildings, but an interesting collection of medieval tombstones etc. can be seen in the present friary garden.

William de Burgo founded the Franciscan friary in Galway in 1296. It later became a place for special theological studies. The Conventuals contested the taking over of Galway friary by the Observants. The co-operation of the local officials enabled the friars to escape suppression and to live in relative peace until 1583, when they were expelled. On their return in 1612, they probably settled on the present site, but were again expelled by the Cromwellians. They returned once again in 1660 and were able to maintain a community there all through the hard times of the eighteenth century (four in 1724, thirteen in 1766, six in 1801). Work on a new church began in 1781, but the present building was not finished until about 1836, and not consecrated until 1849. The friary in its present form dates from 1820. The church is reputed to be the first in Ireland which was dedicated to the Immaculate Conception. The area around the 'Abbey' became the first Franciscan parish in modern Ireland in 1971.

GALWAY COLLEGE (city)

With the rapid expansion of the Irish Franciscan Province in the 1920's, it became necessary to make better arrangements for the education of students. It was decided that they would attend U.C.G. from 1932 on. The foundation stone of a permanent student house, the present St Anthony's College, was laid in 25th. April 1933. A new wing was added in 1941 to allow for the 'student explosion' caused by the closure of the college in Louvain and the impossibility of sending new students to Rome during World War II.

GOLEEN (Co. Cork)

This site is the probable location of the friary of Gahannyh.

Little is known about this foundation other than that it was under repair by Friar Donald O'Scully in 1442.

GOREY (Co. Wexford)

There are no remains of the friars' residence, but the nuns' convent still stands.

The Ram family invited the Franciscan Sisters of Perpetual Adoration to settle in Gorey and some Belgian Franciscans were invited to come along as chaplains. Permission was given for the foundation on 11th. September 1858. The real aim of the Belgian friars was to reform the Irish Franciscans by their example. When the bishop would not grant them the privilege of having a public church, the Belgians moved to Killarney. They left Gorey on 9th. July 1860.

GORMANSTON (Co. Meath)

The Preston family had links with the Irish Franciscans going back to Flanders in the seventeenth century, when the Irish friars were chaplains to the Regiment of Preston. Gormanston Castle was the ancestral home of the family, and it was purchased by the Irish friars in 1947. After some years of hesitation, it was decided to move the Seraphic College (second level boarding school) from Multyfarnham and build a new school at Gormanston. The first pupils arrived on 10th. September 1954, but the transfer was not completed until September 1956. A formal opening by the bishop of Meath, Dr Kyne, in the presence of Cardinal d'Alton, who gave the oration, took place on the memorial day of Fr Luke Wadding (18th. November) in 1956. It had been intended to dedicate the college to the memory of this great Franciscan scholar, but it was thought more fitting to dedicate it to the Immaculate Conception. Construction of the school was finished in September 1957, and of the chapel in 1960. A special language laboratory was opened in 1965. The school now caters for about four hundred and fifty students each year.

JAMESTOWN (Co. Leitrim)

The remains of a small church associated with the friars still stand by the river.

In its origins, Jamestown was a planters' town, so it is unlikely that the friars took up residence there until after its capture by the Irish in 1642. The friars were certainly there by 1644. In August 1650 the friary was the site of a national synod which condemned Ormond and his political associates. It would seem that Fr Bernard Egan continued to work in the area during the Cromwellian period. He later became Minister Provincial and held the Chapters of 1660 and 1661 there. After this the friars maintained strong links with the area. As late as 1801 there was a community of four, probably in Drumreilly Lower. The last friar of Jamestown was probably Fr

Anthony Dunne, who died before 1825. The Franciscan Brothers of the Third Order Regular had a school there at about the same time. This seems to have closed by 1835.

KILCONNELL (Co. Galway)
The site is just on the northern side of the village.
Remains: the church is complete, with tower and transept chapel; the east range of the convent and some sections of the cloister remain; N.B.— two excellent flamboyant tombs in the nave, several carvings, in particular an owl, under the tower; a wooden statue of Our Lady also exists.

Despite some evidence to the contrary, Kilconnell friary was founded by William O'Kelly, Lord of Uí Máine, in 1414. The Observant reform was introduced before 1464. The friary is unusual in that it seems to have escaped suppression right up to the Cromwellian period, although the friars had to abandon the building for short periods. A strong local tradition places their final departure just before the Battle of Aughrim in 1691, but this is rather unlikely. In fact they were working in the area during most of the eighteenth century — there were two at Monabraithre in 1709, ten in 1766. Some of these friars ministered as diocesan clergy. By 1801 it would seem that the last friar had left.

KILCREA (Co. Cork)
The site is near Farran on the Cork to Bantry road.
Remains:both church and convent are almost complete, although some of the cut stone has been removed; a small ivory crucifix from Kilcrea is kept in Cork friary.

One of the early Observant foundations, the friars came to Kilcrea on the invitation of Cormac MacCarthy, Lord of Muskerry, in 1465. The house was protected from suppression by the MacCarthys and the friars were able to remain in residence until a raid by the English authorities in 1578, when two soldiers were killed in a fight over the spoils. When a permanent garrison was established in Kilcrea Castle (1599), the friars had to withdraw for a while, but had returned by 1603. They were finally expelled in 1614. The friars continued to work from their places of hiding. The Anglican Bishop of Cork could complain, in 1731, of the friars who 'creep into the houses of the weak and ignorant people, confirming the Papists in their errors'. By 1766, the remaining friars had withdrawn to Cork city, from where they continued to do occasional work in the Kilcrea region at least as late as 1815.

KILCULLEN (Co. Kildare)
The site is that of the New Abbey Graveyard, about a mile south of the village.

Remains: while most of the stone was removed during building of New Abbey House, part of the old friary was converted into a little catholic chapel in Penal times; low walls mark the outline of this building, which was knocked down about a century ago; a tomb of the founder of the friary, Roland FitzEustace, Baron of Porrlester, and his wife, Margaret Janico, is in the graveyard; there is another in St Audoen's church (C of I), Dublin.

Founded in 1486 for the Observants, the friary of Kilcullen was officially suppressed in 1539. The friars were able to remain in residence until 1547, when they left the area. They made an unsuccessful attempt to return in 1554 and seem to have made no real attempt to take up residence in the area again, except for a short period in the 1640's.

KILDARE (town)
The site is in Grey Abbey graveyard, a little to the south of the town.
Remains: parts of the walls of the choir and nave.

The traditional burial place of the Earls of Kildare, the friary was founded by one George FitzMaurice about 1254-60. With the help of Joan de Burgo, large scale expansion of the buildings took place about 1350. Typical of a community near the Pale, the friars in Kildare accepted the Observant Reform only as late as 1520, while they were among the first communities to be suppressed (1539). The buildings were partially destroyed during a raid by the O'Connors in the following year, and were finally abandoned in 1547. The friars returned to the area in 1621 and continued to work there for about a hundred and fifty years, except during the Cromwellian period.

KILKENNY (city)
The site, recently excavated and tidied up, is in the grounds of a local brewery.
Remains: only the tower and choir may be seen; excavation revealed that the original building was almost identical with Castledermot friary; there is a good sedelia in the choir, excellent finials under the tower, a respond nearby; note also the tomb of the Franciscan bishop, Dr Ledrede, in St Canice's Cathedral.

Although it was founded by the Marshall family about 1232, Kilkenny friary underwent large-scale expansion and re-building early in the fourteenth century. The community remained Conventual right up to the Reformation, followed by suppression in 1540. The friars were expelled from the city in 1550, but managed to return from 1553 to 1559. The Observant friars came to Kilkenny in 1612. When Fr John Dalton ofm. was caught and hanged by the Cromwellians in August 1653, he was the last priest in the city. The friars returned and resumed their normal activities after the

93

Restoration. They became involved in parish work during the eighteenth century and there were still three friars working in the diocese of Ossory in 1801. The last friar of Kilkenny, Fr Philip Forrestall, died in 1829 after many years of parish work.

KILLARNEY (Co. Kerry)

The physical design of the building is based on Muckross friary; note the Flemish-style woodwork in the church.

When the Belgian friars left Gorey in 1860, they settled in Killarney at the invitation of the bishop of Kerry, Dr Moriarty. The memory of the last friars of Muckross was still fresh in the minds of the people. The Belgians were looking for an ideal friary which would be an example for the Irish Franciscans. The bishop was looking for ideal friars who would be a re-incarnation of the spirit of Muckross. The site, Martys's Hill, was where Fr Cornelius MacCarthy had been put to death in 1652 and Fr Thaddeus Moriarty O.P. in 1653. The foundation stone of the new church was laid on 17th. March 1864. Killarney became part of the newly erected English Franciscan custody in 1887, and of the new English Province in 1891, by which time it was serving as the English novitiate. Transferred to the Irish Province in 1902, it soon became the Irish novitiate, which it has remained ever since.

KILLEENAGALLIVE (Co. Tipperary)

There are no remains on the site, which is on the Tipperary-Limerick border, near Emly.

This friary was founded for the Third Order by King Edward IV before 1461. It may have been used by the First Order from 1615 to 1625 and again from 1676 to 1690.

KILLEIGH (Co. Offaly)

One wall of the church remains, just outside the village on the Tullamore road.

Possibly founded by O'Conor Fallighe in 1293, the friary of Killeigh was still Conventual when it was plundered by Lord Grey in 1537-38. The friars managed to remain as a community until about 1580. Individual friars lived on until the Observants came to set up a proper community once again in 1632. While in hiding during the Cromwellian period, the Guardian of Killeigh became Vicar Provincial, but he died before the information reached him. The community emerged into the open again in 1658. By the following century they had become involved in parish work. In 1770-80 there were two friars trying to revive the friary while living at Cully. Fr John Egan died as parish priest of Eglish in 1807. Fr J. J. Donovan was active in the Killurin area about 1821, trying to found a Franciscan school. While he was a member of the Athlone community between 1825 and 1847, he was always interested in reviving an Offaly friary.

KILLINEY (Co. Dublin)

Negotiations were opened in 1941 for the purchase of a house at Seafield Road from Miss Field. It was intended that the community there would engage in higher studies in Irish history and language, as well as Franciscan history. Dún Mhuire was officially opened in April 1945, although the community were not able to settle in for another year. Extended in 1955 and erected into a guardianate in 1975, Dún Mhuire enjoys considerable standing in the academic world.

KILNALAHAN (Co. Galway)

The site is in the village of Abbey on the Clare-Galway border.
Remains: part of the church, with two chapels; sections of other walls.

This was the only Irish Carthusian foundation. The monks were invited in by John de Cogan (see under Claregalway) about 1252. It would seem that this particular order did not suit the Irish temperament since we find them selling most of their temporalities to the Knights Hospitallers in 1306. The decision to let the Irish Charter die was taken by the General Chapter of the Order in 1321, but it was 1341 before the Carthusians had finally departed.

In 1371, the Archbishop of Tuam notes that the monks would have no objection to friars taking possession of the monastery. By 1400 the Franciscans were busy repairing the building. Protected by the Clanricarde family, the friars managed to remain in residence until the end of the sixteenth century, when they had to move due to the destruction of the building. The Observant reform was introduced in 1611. Except during the Cromwellian period, the community were in residence throughout the seventeenth century, but departed in 1698, due to the act banishing religious from Ireland. The friars returned at least as early as early as 1711. There was a community of five in 1766, but the last friar had left by the end of the eighteenth century.

LIMERICK (City)

Nothing remains on the medieval site at the back of Sir Harry's Mall.

Although the earliest certain date in the history of Limerick friary is 1267, with Thomas de Burgo as the founder, it is likely that the friars first arrived in the city about 1245. Situated in the 'English town', the community did not adopt the Observant reform until 1534. The friars went into hiding after the Suppression, but the area around their old building still retained the name 'St Francis Abbey', and the river came to be called 'The Abbey River'.

The friars were able to re-establish a formal residence in 1615, with a community of four. On 14th. June 1646, the standards which had been captured at the Battle of Benburb were displayed in the friary chapel before being deposited in St Mary's Cathedral. The Franciscans were expelled from the city in October 1651, but they soon returned and even managed to recover possession of their little chapel in 1687. In 1732 there were four friars in a small residence near the corner of Nicholas St and Athlunkard St. By 1766, two friars were also doing parish work in the chapels of St Nicholas and of St Mary. In 1782 the community were able to obtain a site in Newgate Lane, where a small friary and chapel were erected. The Franciscans were forced to leave this site in 1822. They settled in Bank Place for a short time, before acquiring the present (Henry St) site in 1824. The chapel was ready in 1826 and the friary in 1827. Both buildings were condemned by the Visitator General in 1873. Work on new buildings began in 1876 and both friary and chapel were open by 1886. However the church was only partially finished and work on the final extension etc. began in 1928. It was consecrated by the Bishop of Limerick, Dr Keane, on 7th. December 1931.

LISGOOLE (Co. Fermanagh)
There are no remains on this site on the southern bank of Upper Lough Erne.

The Canons Regular of St Augustine took possession of the site of the old Irish monastery of St Aid about 1145, and built the Abbey of Sts Peter, Paul and Mary. This building was burned in 1360 and later re-built. Like many other religious houses in Ulster, it escaped suppression. By 1583 the community had dwindled. The Abbot, Cahill Mc'Brien Mc'Cuchonnaght Maguire, drew up an agreement, witnessed by many of the Ulster leaders, to hand the abbey over to the Franciscans. It would seem that the friars had not finished reconstructing the building when they were forced to leave in 1598. They returned in 1616 and served in the region through most of the seventeenth and well into the eighteenth centuries. The gradual involvement of the friars in parish work brought about the dispersal of the community. The last Franciscan to live in the area was Fr Stephen Keenan, who died at Enniskillen in 1811. (See also under Monaghan)

LISLAUGHLIN (Co. Kerry)
The site is on the southern bank of the Shannon Estuary, near Ballylongford.

Remains: Church and transept chapel fairly complete, but tower has

96

fallen; large sections of the friary are also standing; a processional cross belonging to the friary is now in the National Museum of Ireland.

The Observant friars were invited to this part of Kerry by a John O'Connor about 1464. The community lived in peace until three of them were killed by Protestant raiders in 1580. The friars fled and did not return to the area until 1629. Later in the same year, persecution forced some of the friars of Muckross to seek refuge with those who had returned to Lislaughlin. The building was sacked by the Cromwellians in 1652 and the friars were forced into hiding. They came out into the open again about 1660, but seem to have finally abandoned the area early in the eighteenth century.

LOUGH DERG (Co. Donegal)

The history of this site of pilgrimage is complicated. There was an old Irish monastery on the present Station Island. From about 1130 on, the Canons Regular of St Augustine took charge, but moved the pilgrimage to Saints Island, where they remained right down to the Reformation. The Canons then ran into problems of staffing the sanctuary. In 1631 the Archbishop of Armagh officially requested that the Franciscans be given charge of the shrine. There is some evidence to indicate that friars were working at Lough Derg before this.

The Franciscans continued in charge all during the Cromwellian period and well into the following century. At some time, they changed from Saints Island back to Station Island. About 1763 they built a small friary and oratory dedicated to Our Lady of the Angels — the title of the famous Franciscan church at Assisi. In 1780 work began on a church dedicated to St Patrick, but the very next year falling vocations forced the friars to hand over the shrine to the clergy of the diocese of Clogher.

MEELICK (Co. Galway)

The site is about four miles from the village of Eyrecourt.

Remains: church and sacristy are still in use; traces of transept chapel and friary; a small mill; N.B. — bas-relief of St Francis, many seventeenth century inscriptions etc.

Papal permission for Meelick friary was granted by John XXII in 1414, probably on the basis of an O'Madden request. Repair work was being carried out in 1445 and again in 1479, when the friary became Observant. Under O'Madden protection, the friars were able to survive suppression until 1559. They then went into hiding, perhaps in the Wood of Muckeny, or on Friars Island. However they were never very far away from their old home, and returned as soon as they could. The friars again made preparations to depart in 1698,

97

but soon returned. There were four friars in the community at Meelick during most of the eighteenth century. In addition many friars worked in the parishes of Fahy and Meelick. By the nineteenth century, the community had dwindled to two, despite which the church was repaired in 1832. The last friar of Meelick was Fr Bonaventure Francis Reynolds. When he died in November 1852, there was no friar available to replace him.

MONAGHAN (1) (town)
The exact site is uncertain and there are no significant remains.

Monaghan was the site of one of the late Conventual foundations, about 1462. The MacMahons protected the friars. Although it had suffered an attack in 1540, the friary was not evacuated until it was sacked by an English army in 1589, by which time the community had become Observant. The friars returned about 1635 and, apart from the Cromwellian period, continued to reside in the town for most of that century. In the first half of the eighteenth century the community gradually dispersed and became involved in parish activity.

MONAGHAN (2) (parish activity in the diocese of Clogher)
As the communities associated with the friaries of Monaghan and Lisgoole began to disperse towards the middle of the eighteenth century, the friars became more involved in parish work. As late as 1801 fifteen Franciscans were working in the diocese in areas such as Ballybay, Donaghmore, Lough Egish and Aughnamullen. The last friars associated with the area would be Fr Thomas Martin, who worked around Ballytrain and died in 1849-50, and Fr John McMahon, who lived at Chapel Moyle (Lough Egish) about 1845.

MONASTERORIS (Co. Offaly)
The site is in a graveyard about 4 kms. west of Edenderry.
Remains: most of the church, altered and overgrown with ivy.

The name of this friary comes from the Irish version of the founder's name — John de Bermingham, Earl of Louth (MacFeoris — Monaster Feoris) — who brought the friars there in 1325. The Observant reform was adopted in 1506. While in use as a fort by the Irish, the building was severely damaged during a siege by the Lord Lieutenant in 1521. The friars were able to remain in the area for about another fifty years. They returned to the site of their old foundation about 1645. After the expulsion of the friars in Cromwellian times, there is little evidence of Franciscan activity in the area until the eighteenth century, when the friars took on parish work in the Rhode — Daingean area. We may regard Fr Matthew Walsh, vicar of Daingean, who died in 1794, as the last friar of Monasteroris.

MONS PIETATIS (Co. Mayo)

This mysterious friary, somewhere in Co. Mayo, first appears in official documents in 1645, implying a foundation about 1643. Papal approval was sought in 1663 and a superior was appointed in 1672. This is the last real evidence for a Franciscan connection, although the name remained in use during the eighteenth century. Given a strong local tradition, Killedan, west of Kiltamagh, seems the most likely site.

MOYNE (Co. Mayo)

The site is on the shore of Killala Bay and should be visited in conjunction with the neighbouring Third Order friary of Rosserk.
Remains: church, chapels, tower and friary are practically complete.

Moyne was the first proper foundation of the Observant friars in 1460, although it had been built a few years before (see Chapter 3). The de Burgos were the major patrons and the church was consecrated in 1462. Building continued for another fifty years. By this time Moyne had become a student house and had a community of about fifty. Typical of a friary in an Irish area, it escaped early suppression. Despite problems in 1578-9, the building was not destroyed nor the community dispersed until it was raided by Sir Richard Bingham in 1590. About six friars remained and they were able to re-open a formal residence in 1618. There they lived for the rest of the century, except during 1550-8. After the efforts to expel the religious from Ireland in 1697, the friars seem to have moved to Kilmacshalgan (Co. Sligo), at least for a while, and became involved in parish work. The community of six in 1744 was reduced to two by 1771 and the last friar of Moyne, Fr Thomas Burke, died in 1800. The friars considered returning to the area in 1913.

MUCKROSS (als. Irrelagh) (Co. Kerry)

The site is a well-known tourist attraction by the Lakes of Killarney.
Remains: the church, transept chapel, tower and friary are complete.

Donal McCarthy Mór founded the friary of Muckross for the Observant friars about 1448. Building continued for nearly fifty years. The friary was dedicated to the Holy Trinity. The community was legally suppressed in 1541, but the friars were able to remain in residence until about 1589, when two friars were killed during an English raid. The Franciscans returned about 1600, again about 1612, and at least by 1639, having been driven out on the two previous occasions. The Cromwellians expelled them again in 1652. The friars withdrew to a place of refuge, probably Friars Glen on the side of Mangerton. About 1760 the few remaining friars moved to a cottage at Faghbawn, by the Flesk river. By now the community was reduced to two, yet the friars started a college in 1780 on the site of

99

the present Scott's Hotel in Killarney. This eventually grew into the diocesan college of St Brendan. The last friar, Fr J. FitzGerald, probably left Killarney in 1849. When the Belgian friars came to Kerry in 1860, Fr FitzGerald was guardian of Waterford friary. He died at Athlone in 1880.

MULTYFARNHAM (Co. Westmeath)
The site is that of the present Franciscan friary.
Remains: the nave, transept chapel and tower are original; the choir and some of the windows are modern.

The origins of the friary of Multyfarnham are obscure. Founded by the Delamars between 1250 and 1265, the early community received much help from the Nugents. The friars adopted the Observant reform at an early stage. The friary was suppressed in October 1540, but the friars were able to live on under Nugent protection. By 1600 the community numbered eighteen and was one of the largest in Ireland. In a vicious raid on 1st. October 1601, Sir Francis Shane destroyed the building and captured eleven of the community. From then until about 1622 the Franciscans of Multyfarnham were subjected to continual harassment. The friars went into hiding during 1651-9 and set up a residence at Knightswood, where there was a community of about ten in 1671. From 1700 on, the friars were involved in parish work and were able to return to their original building in 1710. The last Franciscan parish priest of Multyfarnham, Fr Edward Francis Dease, died in 1824. Part of the medieval chapel was restored in 1827, and a small residence built on the ruins of the old convent in 1839. On 11th. December 1896 the 'brown' Franciscans took over Multyfarnham as the first reform house in Ireland (see Chapter 8). Plans were made to open a seraphic college, where candidates for the Order could be educated. St Louis College thus came into being in 1899. When this college was moved to Gormanston in 1956, Multyfarnham became St Isidore's Agricultural College. There have been extensive alterations to the church at Multyfarnham in recent years, both to increase its pastoral effectiveness and to restore its medieval flavour.

NENAGH (Co. Tipperary)
The site is on a lane to the south of the main street.
Remains: the church is complete, but the tower has fallen.

With O'Kennedy sponsorship, Nenagh friary was probably founded before 1252. In later times, it became the head-house of the Irish custody within the Province (see Chapter 2). The O'Carrolls burned the town of Nenagh, including the still-Conventual friary, in 1548. The friars seem to have lived on until about 1587, after which no effort was made to set up a residence until 1632, when the

Observants came. The friars were expelled by the Cromwellians, but soon returned. A community was still in residence in the early eighteenth century, but had broken up by 1766. There were still friars working as parish clergy in the area and Fr Patrick Harty died there in 1817 as a quasi-cutate. He was the last Franciscan of Nenagh.

NEW ROSS(Co. Wexford)
Nothing now remains on the site, although some tomb-slabs from the friary have been re-erected at St Mary's Church.

The Earl of Pembroke made a foundation in New Ross for the Crossed Friars about 1195, while the Franciscan Friars came to the town about 1250. When a drunken Crossed Friar killed a townsman, the citizens drove his Order from the town and gave their building to the Franciscans. The community remained Conventual right up to 1558, when the friars were finally expelled after a number of false alarms. The Observants came and set up a residence in 1615. Expelled during the Cromwellian period, the friars soon returned and remained for another century, finally departing about 1750.

QUIN (Co. Clare)
The site is on the edge of the village, behind the Catholic church. **Remains:** church, tower, transept chapel, friary and some outbuildings are complete; note how the ruins of the old castle have been skillfully incorporated into the friary, also the gigantic tomb of the Butlers of Dunboyne in the room beside the refectory.

Quin was founded for the Observants on the basis of permission obtained by Sioda Cam MacNamara in 1433. It was built on the ruins of a de Clare castle founded in 1280. Under O'Brien protection, the friars were able to live on after the Suppression. Despite the partial destruction of the building in 1583, the friars did not depart, but repaired the damage. There was a small community of three living there in 1615. Three friars were killed in an attack on the building in 1651, after which the remaining friars withdrew for a couple of years. On their return, the friars worked in Quin until about 1740, when they moved to a house at near-by Drim. There were three friars at Drim in 1766, working as parish clergy. The last friar of Quin, Fr John Hogan, worked at Drim until his death in 1820.

ROSCOMMON (town)
The friars were invited to Roscommon in 1269, but had to leave the following year when their house was destroyed by fire and their benefactor had died.

ROSCREA (Co. Tipperary)
The site is the entrance gate to the grounds of the catholic church. **Remains:** the tower still stands, as do large sections of the church.

Roscrea was a late Conventual foundation, before 1477. The

actual building dates to 1490-8, sponsored by Molrony O'Carroll and his wife, Bibiana. The community escaped suppression until 1579, when two friars were captured during an English raid. One was killed, the other abandoned his religion. He was re-converted by Fr Donagh Mooney during a mission and returned to the friars until his death. An Observant residence was set up in Roscrea about 1645 and lasted for about a hundred years, except during times of persecution (1650-8 and again in 1670-89).

ROSS (Rosseriall Friary, Co. Galway)

The site is in a bog about a mile west of the village of Headford. Remains: the church, tower, chapels and friary are almost complete; there is evidence for large-scale alterations in the eighteenth century.

Little is certain about the early history of Ross friary. A reasonable guess is that it was founded in 1498 for the Observants. Protected by the Clanricarde family, the friars were able to remain on after the Suppression despite several plunderings. In 1616 there was a community of six priests and two brothers in the old building. An unusual incident occured during 1641, when the guardian saved the survivors of an English party of travellers who had been attacked by the Irish near Shrule. The Cromwellian period meant some time in hiding for the friars. The friary was sacked in 1656. The friars had returned by 1661 and did not leave again until the attempted general expulsion of religious in 1697. They had come back again by 1711, when their protector was Lord St George. At some stage they had withdrawn to Friars Island, but now, through the generosity of a Mr Lynch, the friars were able to build a new home for themselves at the foot of Kilroe Hill. There was a community of seven living at Kilroe in 1766, but this had fallen to three by 1801. There were still three friars in the community when the friary was closed by order of the Provincial in 1832.

ROSSNOWLAGH (Co. Donegal)

During the celebrations in 1944, to mark the Third Centenary of the death of Br Michael O'Cleary the idea was mooted that the Franciscans should return to Donegal. Encouraged by the local bishop, Dr MacNeely, the friars took up the suggestion. A site was chosen in 1946 near Br Michael's own area of Kilbarron. The first community lived in Nissen huts until the new friary and church were ready. These were officially blessed and dedicated on 29th. June 1952. The friary became a full guardianate in 1954 and has since established a Franciscan presence over a huge surrounding area. At the moment the friars also have temporary charge of the parish of Ballintra.

102

SHERKIN ISLAND (Co. Cork)

There is a regular boat service to the island from Baltimore.
Remains: church, tower and transept still stand, as does most of the convent; however some inner walls have been knocked down.

Permission for this foundation was given by Rome to Finighin O'Driscoll in 1449, but it was not until just after 1462 that the Observant friars actually arrived. The friary became the traditional burial place of the O'Driscolls. In 1537 the citizens of Waterford burned the building in retaliation for acts of piracy by the O'Driscolls. The great bell of the friary was on display in Waterford as late as 1615. There is no evidence to suggest that the friars were disturbed by the events of the Reformation until the island was garrisoned by the English following the Battle of Kinsale. The friars soon returned and, except at the height of the Cromwellian persecution, were active all during the seventeenth and well into the eighteenth centuries. The last friar, Fr Patrick Hayes, died soon after 1766.

SLANE (Co. Meath)

The site was the little church and hermitage of St Erc.

In addition to a Third Order friary and a college with Capuchin associations on the Hill of Slane itself, there is evidence for a small Franciscan First Order community in the hermitage during 1648-50.

STRABANE (Co. Tyrone)

There is some evidence for a friary a few miles east of the town from the time of the Restoration (1660's) to early in the eighteenth century. The foundation cannot have been very large or significant.

STRADBALLY (Co. Laois)

There are no signficant remains on the site at the back of the Convent school.

The early history of the friars in Stradbally is confusing. The building was erected by Lord O'Moore about 1447 for the Conventual friars. The friary escaped suppression until 1569, probably due to its small size. The community went into hiding. Three of them were discovered in 1588 and were hung, drawn and quartered near Abbeyleix. Two friars returned to the area in 1642, but were forced to leave during the Cromwellian persecution. There seems to have been no really serious effort to return to the area after this.

STRADE (Co. Mayo)

John of Exeter invited the Franciscan friars here in 1252, but that same year his wife, Basilia (a daughter of Meiler de Bermingham) persuaded him to transfer the foundation to the Dominicans.

THURLES (town)

The friars of Cashel were renting a house in Thurles from the Matthews family in 1714. By 1740 the community seems to have moved permanently from Cashel to Thurles. There were usually two or three friars living in a small cottage with a private oratory. There was no public church. The friars helped out at the Cathedral. The most famous friar in Thurles during the last century was Fr James (Theodosius) McNamara, who lived there from 1834 to his death in 1881. Efforts to close the residence in Thurles in 1859 were strongly resisted by the archbishop. By then the friars had become chaplains to the workhouse. A decision to close the house was taken at the Provincial Chapter in 1892 and the last friar of Thurles, Fr Pacificus Doggette, was moved to Multyfarnham.

TIMOLEAGUE (Co. Cork)

The site is on a headland beside the village.

Remains: church, tower, transept and aisle are complete; large sections of the friary still stand; including parts of the cloister arcade.

Many people associate Timoleague friary with the Irish poem by Seán O Coileáin 'Oidhche dham go doiligh, dubhach . . .', which is a translation from the English poem by Fr Matthew Horgan. The friary of Tigh-mo-Laghi dates back to about 1307. It owes its origins to the combined efforts of Donal Glas MacCarthy and William de Barry. The building underwent continuous expansion, e.g. the tower was added about 1510. It was one of the first Franciscan communities to adopt the Observant reform in 1460-1. Protected by Cormac McCarthy Reagh, the friars were able to remain in residence right up to the Cromwellian period. They had, of course, to flee several times when the friary itself was plundered, the last occasion being as late as 1642. After the Restoration, they emerged from their place of hiding at Clogagh. Although the community had dispersed by the middle of the eighteenth century, individual friars continued to work in the area. The last of these was Fr Bonaventure Tobin, who died about 1822.

TRIM (Co. Meath)

There are no remains at this site near the bridge over the Boyne river.

While the first certain date for the Franciscan friary at Trim is 1318, we may be fairly sure that the friars arrived as early as 1282. In 1330 (and again about 1430) the buildings were badly damaged by Boyne floods. The community adopted the Observant reform before 1506. The friars were expelled from Trim in 1542 and did not return until 1629. By the eighteenth century, they had become involved in parish work on a large scale (see under Courtown).

WATERFORD (city)

The medieval site, known as 'The French Church' is about a quarter of a mile from the present friary.

Remains: the church, tower and parts of the transept chapel are complete; N.B. — the collection of medieval statues from the friary kept in the Holy Ghost Hospital.

Waterford friary was one of the first in Ireland, being founded by Hugh Purcell about 1240. It was the scene of the surrender of four Irish chieftains (the O'Conor Don, de Burgo, O'Brien and O'Kennedy) to Richard II in 1395. The community did not adopt the Observant reform until 1521. The friary was suppressed on 2nd. April 1540, but the friars were able to remain in the city. Henry VIII granted a charter in 1544 to convert part of the building into a hospital-cum-alms-house, this being the original Holy Ghost Hospital. The church was used for burials, then (in 1693) by some French Huguenots, and later by the Methodists. These latter afterwards built a church on the site of the convent.

Following suppression, the friars moved into hiding in Johnstown, although some of them acted as chaplains to the Holy Ghost Hospital. An official residence was set up in 1612. The friars were forced out of the town in 1652, but returned to Johnstown in 1660. From then on the community numbered two or three. Not having a public church, the priests helped in the parish church. In addition individual friars became parish clergy in other parts of the diocese. The residence was changed to the area of South Parade and Water St about 1790. The friars moved to their present site in 1830 and opened a small chapel and residence in 1835. The church was expanded in 1905-8 and again in 1931-3. It was consecrated in 1944. The present friary was built in 1928.

WEXFORD (town)

Nothing remains of the medieval building, which was on the present site.

Little is known of the early history of Wexford friary. It was founded about 1265 and the community adopted the Observant reform in 1486. After the friary was suppressed in 1540, the friars went into hiding. A small residence was set up in 1615 and a thatched chapel was opened in 1620, both in High St. Seven members of the community were killed when the Cromwellians broke into Wexford in 1649. Another four friars were killed in 1655. The community was able to return in 1660 and the chapel was re-opened in 1673. A new church was ready on the old medieval site in 1690 and it was the only church open in Wexford during the long Penal period. The first of the new parish churches was opened in 1858. It was only natural that the friars became involved in parish work under these circumstances. They ran an academy, or secondary school, for a while early in the nineteenth century. This was replaced by the present St Peter's College. Down the years the seventeenth century church underwent frequent alterations, especially about 1790 and in 1857. The friary was built in 1803 and served both as the residence of the Provincial and as the novitiate for much of the first half of the nineteenth century. The Brown friars introduced the reform into Wexford in 1918.

WICKLOW (town)
The site is in the garden of the parish priest.
Remains: parts of the church and transept.

Expert opinion dates the friary of Wicklow to about 1265, while oral tradition tells us that it was built in thanksgiving for a victory over the FitzGeralds by the O'Tooles and O'Byrnes. It is not certain when the community adopted the Observant reform, nor when the friars had to leave the district. By 1615, we know that the area had been long deserted by the friars. They returned about 1635, were expelled by the Cromwellians, and returned again in 1659. However the new community was not energetic and Franciscan life in Wicklow died out early in the eighteenth century.

YOUGHAL (Co. Cork)
The site is now occupied by the Presentation Convent. There are no significant remains.

Tradition has it that the first friars to arrive in Ireland landed at Youghal and that their first foundation was made in the town. Work on a permanent building began under the patronage of MauriceFitzGerald, Justiciar of Ireland, about 1235. The friary was the scene of an unusual incident when the sheriff raided it to seize goods which had been left in the safe keeping of the friars. This was done to pay the taxes of the owner of the goods, John le Juvene. In 1460 Youghal became one of the first houses to adopt the Observant reform. The friars were able to remain in or near their old building until 1583, when it was destroyed by the English. The community probably withdrew to a place of refuge at Curraheen, but were able to re-establish a residence in Youghal in 1627. Forced out by the Cromwellians, the friars soon returned. However the difficulties of living in Youghal during the Penal period forced them to move to Co. Waterford (see under Curraheen).

Cashel Friary:
Lady

Knight

107

SITES IN ENGLAND OR ON THE CONTINENT

BALLABEG (Bymacan, Isle of Man)
The site is on a farm just outside the village.

Remains: most of the church and parts of the friary.

Since there was no other Franciscan foundation in the diocese of Sodor, Urban V granted the Irish friars permission for a foundation at Ballabeg on 7th. December 1367. William Montague, Earl of Salisbury, had invited the friars, so that they could look after the people on a neglected part of his estates. Permission was granted to consecrate the church in 1373. The initial community numbered twelve friars. In later years, two Irish friars became bishops of Man. The community seem to have dispersed and ceased to function following the suppression of the friary in 1540.

BOULAY (Lorraine, France)
The site is to the north of the main square.
Remains: parts of some walls and large sections of the gardens.

A château, at Boulay, which belonged to the Duke of Lorraine, was ruined by fire in 1695. The Act expelling religious from Ireland was just about to become law. Two Irish friars, Frs Bernardine Gavan and Bernardine Plunket, independently discovered that the Duke was sympathetic to an Irish foundation. Strict conditions imposed by the Bishop of Metz had discouraged German friars, but Fr Plunket applied for permission to make a foundation in 1698. The legalities took two years to complete and it was not until 1700 that the Irish Franciscans could take over the ruined building. The initial community of six grew to about twenty five and the château was slowly converted into a college. Thus what was the great hall became the refectory. In addition to its role as an Irish student house, the college at Boulay became a centre for local pastoral action and the friars ran a school for the local youth. Two thirds of the community had to speak German. During the French Revolution, soldiers were billeted in the college in 1790. It was then turned into a place of retirement for elderly religious. It was finally closed for Catholic use in October 1792. After the Revolution efforts were made to recover the college, but lack of finance proved a major difficulty. Money to compensate the friars got lost in a bureaucratic wrangle between the British and French governments.

CAPRANICA (Province of Viterbo, Italy)
The old buildings are still in use by the Irish Franciscans.

The church here was built in 1551 by the Society of Hunters to house the picture of Our Lady painted by Andrea Vanni about 1340.

The Hermits of St Augustine took over the church in 1559 and added the convent. They let the whole building go to ruin and it partially collapsed in 1632, as a result of which they abandoned it in 1652.

Fr Luke Wadding, the founder of St Isidore's College in Rome, was looking for a small house outside Rome for the Irish Franciscans. Having first considered San Antonio in Casale, he applied for Capranica and obtained it as a holiday house and novitiate in 1656. The extensive repairs which were necessary took until 1663, by which time the community numbered fifteen. During the eighteen century, there was a small community at Capranica and it still served as a novitiate, in addition to St Isidore's. Lost to the French invaders in 1798, it was not recovered until 1814. It was then rented to a local landlord, who provided a priest to say mass on the major feasts. The revenue from Capranica served to keep St Isidore's open. In 1853 Capranica returned to its original function of being a novitiate, but did not become of major importance until the period of the Doebbing reform. In 1890 Fr Doebbing was appointed delegate general for Capranica and began using it as a house of formation. It also served as a seraphic college for training candidates for the Irish Province. Irish and German friars began an active apostolate in the area. Capranica was returned to full Irish control and, in 1906, the Irish Definitorium made a formal decision to retain it as part of the Irish Province. Since then it has functioned as a holiday house for St Isidore's, with Italian Franciscans staffing the church.

CASTEL SANT'ELIA (Province of Viterbo, Italy)

This former hermitage was taken over by the Irish friars in 1892. Fr Doebbing acted as delegate general. It was used, with Rome and Capranica, to house friars engaged in the reform of the Irish province. The Irish withdrew in 1898 and Sant'Elia became the responsibility of the German Province of Saxony. They have since enlarged the convent and made it a major place of pilgrimage in honour of Our Lady.

LOUVAIN (now Leuven, Belgium)
The College of St Anthony is still in Irish Franciscan hands.

The Irish Minister Provincial, Fr Florence Conry, used his influence with Philip III of Spain to get an Irish Franciscan College in the Low Countries. Permission was given in 1606 and papal approval was granted in 1607. The friars tried a number of places in Louvain before settling on the present site, where the foundation stone of St Anthony's College was laid on 9th. May 1617. Louvain, the first of the Irish Franciscan continental colleges, became an active centre for Irish studies (see Chapter 5). Although the friars of the

Louvain school are best known for their works on Irish history, e.g. the Annals of the Four Masters, they also produced many religious works in Irish. The activities of the college were slightly curtailed by the anti-religious decrees of Emperor Joseph II in 1782. During the French Revolution, the seals of the Republic were attached to the door of the college in 1793. Over the next few years the Guardian, Fr James Cowan, vainly struggled to keep the building in Irish hands. It was finally sold in 1822. Much valuable manuscript material had already been confiscated and still lies in Brussels. The remainder was sent either to Rome or to Wexford.

After a century of use as a school for under-privileged children, the property came on the market again in 1922 and was purchased for the Irish friars in 1925. The first community moved in during 1926, but extensive renovations delayed a formal opening until 30th. June 1927. Due to the German invasion of Belgium, the college was evacuated in May 1940 and given into the charge of the Belgian friars. It was returned to Irish control in 1948 and soon reverted to its normal role as a residence for under-graduate and post-graduate students. Since 1969, friars of the community in Louvain have been providing facilities for English-speaking catholics in Brussels, especially Sunday mass. This arrangement was formalised into a regular chaplaincy in 1972 and the Irish Franciscans have pastoral charge of the English and Irish catholic population in Brussels.

PARIS (France)

The Irish Franciscans sought many times to obtain a residence in Paris for any friar who wished to study at the University. These efforts were opposed by the French friars, who ran an international hostel. There was an Irish Franciscan house in Paris from 1617 for a couple of years, from 1621 to 1627 and again from 1653 to 1668. An attempt by the French government in 1810 to set up an English-speaking seminary, which would include the Irish friars, was a fiasco.

PRAGUE (Czechoslovakia)

Most of the house and the church are still standing on Hybernska.

Fr Malachy Fallon was sent from an over-crowded Louvain to the Emperor at Vienna in 1628 to obtain another Irish Franciscan foundation. He found a suitable site in Prague and in 1630 a group set out for the city to found what became the largest of the Irish Franciscan continental colleges — the College of the Immaculate Conception at Prague. The building was formally opened on 6th. July 1631, but expansion continued. The foundation-stone of a new church was laid in 1652, while extra wings were added to the college in 1704 and in 1739. The college was suppressed by direct order of Emperor Joseph II on 29th. August 1786, at which time there were thirty seven friars in residence. Six old friars were allowed to stay on in Prague, with government pensions, until they died. The buildings became government property and are now used as an exhibition centre.

ROME (Italy)
The College of St Isidore is still used by the Irish Franciscans.

Fr Luke Wadding arrived in Rome on official Spanish business in 1617 and began to look for an Irish Franciscan house in the Eternal City. A group of Spanish Discalced Franciscans had begun the erection of a friary dedicated to St Isidore the Farmer of Madrid in the same year that he had been canonized — 1622. Due to financial problems, the Spanish friars withdrew and went to live at Ara Coeli, the residence of the Minister General. Fr Luke saw his opportunity and the building was granted to the Irish friars by decree of the Minister General on 13th. June 1625. Pope Urban VIII issued the Bull of Foundation on 20th. October. From then until his death in 1657, Fr Luke laboured to expand the college to its present size. He also founded the Irish Pastoral College. Major restoration work was done at St Isidore's about 1750. The building was seized by the invading French in 1798-9 and again in 1810. On this occasion the college was turned into tenements and many of the rooms were let to a group of artists known as the 'Nazarenes'. The guardian, Fr James McCormick, managed to remain in residence and he regained complete control of the college in October 1814. Restoration work was again carried out in 1856 and about 1890. Following the appointment of Fr Bernard Doebbing as lecturer and master at St Isidore's, the college became a centre for the reform of the Irish friars (see Chapter 8). In due time the college reverted to Irish control. Students were normally trained in theology by lecturers living in the college. Since World War II they have begun to attend outside universities in Rome. Although cut off from Ireland during the World War, the college was able to remain active and is still the main house of theological training for the Irish Franciscans.

WIELUN (South-east Poland)
Exact site and present condition unknown: parts believed to exist.

The Irish friars had been seeking a foundation at Danzig or Poznan, but were blocked by the King of Poland. Then the friars of the Province of St Anthony took pity on the Irish and offered them the friary of the Annunciation at Wielun on 16th. July 1645. The loan was approved by the Minister General in 1646 and the first community seems to have come from Louvain. The Polish friars requested the return of their friary in 1653 and the Irish friars seem to have been fairly happy to oblige.

GLOSSARY

black friars: those Franciscans who did not conform to the reform in Ireland at the end of the nineteenth century.

brown friars: the Franciscans who adopted the reform in Ireland at the end of the nineteenth century.

chapter: a meeting of representatives of the friars for the purpose of electing superiors and passing legislation; a general chapter involves the friars of the whole world, a provincial chapter those of a particular province.

chapter bill: a document produced after a provincial chapter which lists new appointments and may indicate changes in legislation.

conferences, theological: regular meetings of priests at which items of a theological nature are discussed with the aim of keeping the clergy abreast of the teaching of the Church on theological matters.

congregation: the title given to a provincial chapter at which major superiors (the provincial and his definitorium) are not elected.

constitutions, general: a basic code of law covering the entire Order.

convent: technically a 'formed house' i.e. with a community of at least six religious living in a house which has been legally erected; used in a wide sense to mean the part of a friary building where the friars actually live; see 'residence'.

Conventual: term applied to the non-reform group within the Order in the sixteenth century, and the name applied to that group after the Order was split into two Orders in 1517; this Order died out in Ireland after the Reformation.

custody: an administrative unit within a province of the Order, governed by a custos; under certain circumstances, it may be independent.

definitor: member of the inner council which advises and guides the minister general or the minister provincial on the running of the order or the province.

erect: legal term covering the formalities of settling up a house in law by obtaining the necessary permissions.

faculties: the permission given by a bishop or a major superior to priests so that they may administer the sacraments, in particular penance, and preach.

foundation: a term governing the permission given in writing by the local bishop by which a convent may be erected in law, and includes permission for a public church; sometimes incorrectly used about permission for a residence.

friary: generally used to mean any place where friars live, be it a convent or a residence.

112

general: the head of the Franciscan Order; the full title is minister general; the vicar general governs the Order in the absence of the minister general, but this has also been used as a title for a person governing large sections of the Order and responsible only to the minister general; the procurator general is the chief adviser to the minister general and handles relations with the Roman Curia; a commissary general and a delegate general are people to whom the minister general has delegated part of his authority to deal with particular problems or special circumstances; for visitator general, see under visitator.

guardian: the superior of a convent, thus giving rise to the term guardianate for such a house; in Ireland a tradition arose by which friars were nominated titular guardians to old convents where there were no longer resident communities.

mission: an organised group of friars living in a foreign country and trying to instill the faith there; or a period of special preaching within a christianised country, with the aim of deepening the faith.

Observant: term applied to the reform group within the Order in the fifteenth century, and the names applied to that group after the Order was split into two Orders in 1517; the use of the term ceased towards 1700; the reform movement is found in other orders but I have used it in a specific Franciscan sense.

province: the Franciscan Order is divided, for administrative purposes, into provinces, each of which is quasi-autonomous; the friar who governs the province is the minister provincial and his assistant is the vicar provincial; this latter title is also used for the friar who rules the province in the absence of the minister provincial, or who governs part of the province in his own right.

president: the superior of a residence.

quest: the seeking of alms from lay people by the friars.

regulars: religious who take solemn vows and thus belong to an order, as distinct from those who take simple vows and belong to a congregation; in practice, those who belong to the monastic orders (monks) or mendicant orders (friars) and who are exempt from the authority of the local bishop.

residence: any house where religious live and which has not been erected into a foundation, either because there is not a sufficient number of religious in the community, or because the local bishop will not permit a full foundation.

Restoration: the period immediately following the restoration of Charles II to the throne in 1660.

Seraphic: the title Seraphic is proper to the Franciscans, just as the title Angelic is proper to the Dominicans; a seraphic college is a minor seminary for training candidates to the Order.

statutes: while constitutions form a code of law proper to the whole Order, laws proper to particular sections of the Order are called statutes.

Suppression: the period during which the buildings belonging to the various orders in Ireland were confiscated by the civil authority and the communities dispersed; in practice, 1536 to about 1550.

visitator: at regular intervals of three or six years, a representative of the general or the provincial himself pays an official visit to all the houses within a province, correcting faults or consulting the friars on various matters.

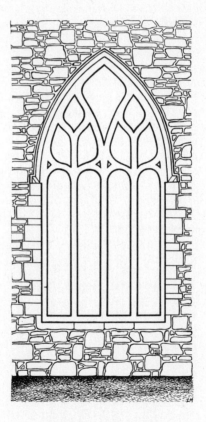

Dromahair Friary: Window

BIBLIOGRAPHY

There is no full history of the Irish Franciscans. Footnotes were not included in this work by reason of its size and scope. The interested reader may fill out his knowledge a little more from these items:

(a) Medieval period:
  BRADSHAW, Brendan: *The Dissolution of the Religious Orders in Ireland*, Cambridge, 1974.
  FITZMAURICE, E. B., ofm., & LITTLE, A. G.: *Materials for the history of the Franciscan Province of Ireland*, (British Society of Franciscan Studies, ix), Manchester, 1920.
  GWYNN, A., & HADCOCK, R. N.: *Medieval Religious Houses in Ireland*, London, 1971.
  MATTHEWS (O'Mahony), F., ofm.: *Brevis synopsis provinciae Hiberniae Fratrum Minorum*, edited in *Analecta Hibernica* 6 (1934), pp. 139-91.
  MOONEY, C., ofm.: *The Franciscans in Ireland*, in *Terminus* viii — xiv (1954-7), *passim.*
  MOONEY, C., ofm.: *Franciscan architecture in pre-Reformation Ireland*, in *R.S.A.I. Jn.*, lxxxv — lxxxvii (1955-7), *passim.*
  MOONEY, D., ofm.: *De provincia Hiberniae S. Francisci*, edited in *Analecta Hibernica* 6 (1934), pp. 12-138.
  WATT, J. A.: *The Church and the Two Nations in Medieval Ireland*, (Cambridge studies in Medieval Life & Thought, 3rd. series, 3), Cambridge, 1970.

(b) The Seventeenth Century:
  GIBLIN, C., ofm., ed.: *Liber Lovaniensis*, Dublin, 1956.
  MILLETT, B., ofm.: *The Irish Franciscans 1651-1665*, (Analecta Gregoriana, vol. 129), Rome, 1964.
  MOONEY, C., ofm.: *The Golden Age of the Irish Franciscans, 1615-50*, in O'Brien, S. ofm., ed.: *Measgra i gcuimhne Mhichíl Uí Chléirigh*, Dublin, 1944, pp. 19-33.

(c) Modern period:

Very little has been published dealing with this period.

CONLAN, P., ofm.: *A short-title calendar of Hibernia, vol. 1(1706-1869) in the General Archives of the Friars Minor, Rome,* in *Collectanea Hibernica,* 18/19(1976-77).

FAULKNER, A., ofm.: an edition of the Chapter Bills up to 1875 is with the printers.

FENNING, H., op.: *The Undoing of the Friars of Ireland*: a study of the novitiate question in the eighteenth century, Louvain, 1972.

MC GRATH, K.: *The Irish Franciscans in the Eighteenth Century*, in *Franciscan College Annual*, Multyfarnham, 1950, pp. 53-8.

MC GRATH, K.: *Sidelights on the Irish Franciscans 1798-1850*, in *Franciscan College Annual*, Multyfarnham, 1952, pp. 81-8.

Kilconnell Friary: Owl

116

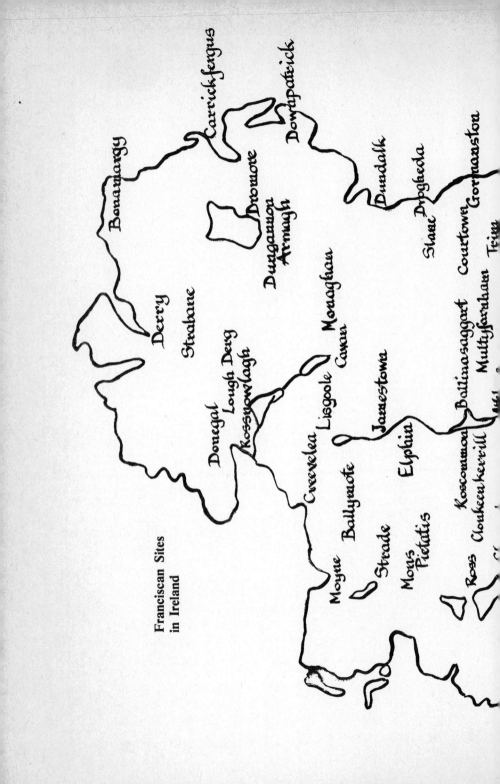

Franciscan Sites
in Ireland